THEY WROTE OUR HYMNS

*by the same author*

THE BEATITUDES
THE CLAIMS OF CHRIST *A Study in His Self-Portraiture*
LUKE'S PORTRAIT OF JESUS
THE MEANING OF THE OLD TESTAMENT
THE PARABLES OF THE GOSPELS
PAUL'S LETTERS TO HIS FRIENDS
PURITANISM AND RICHARD BAXTER
ed.: THE HOLY COMMUNION
ed.: A TREASURY OF CHRISTIAN VERSE
etc.

# THEY WROTE OUR HYMNS

HUGH MARTIN CH, DD

SCM PRESS LTD
BLOOMSBURY STREET LONDON

FIRST PUBLISHED 1961
© SCM PRESS LTD 1961
PRINTED IN GREAT BRITAIN BY
EAST MIDLAND PRINTING COMPANY LIMITED
BURY ST EDMUNDS AND ELSEWHERE

# CONTENTS

|    | INTRODUCTION | 7 |
|----|---|---|
| 1  | SONGS BEFORE UNKNOWN<br>*The achievement of Isaac Watts (1674-1748)* | 9 |
| 2  | HARK THE GLAD SOUND!<br>*Philip Doddridge's hymns to 'fix' the sermon (1702-1751)* | 27 |
| 3  | BORN IN SONG<br>*John (1703-91) and Charles (1707-88) Wesley and the hymns of Methodism* | 41 |
| 4  | GOD'S MYSTERIOUS WAY<br>*The strange stories of William Cowper (1731-1800) and John Newton (1725-1807)* | 57 |
| 5  | STAND UP AND BLESS THE LORD!<br>*James Montgomery (1771-1854), the layman who left an imperishable inheritance* | 81 |
| 6  | IN EVERY PART WITH PRAISE<br>*Horatius Bonar (1808-89), the prince of Scottish hymn-writers* | 95 |
| 7  | THE ROYAL BANNERS<br>*John Mason Neale (1818-66) and the hymns of the Catholic Revival* | 100 |
| 8  | FOR ALL THE SAINTS<br>*William Walsham How (1823-97), the beloved bishop* | 114 |
| 9  | THE DAY THOU GAVEST<br>*John Ellerton (1826-93), the parish priest whose life was devoted to hymns* | 118 |
| 10 | THE CONTRIBUTION OF WOMEN | 126 |
|    | INDEX | 141 |

# INTRODUCTION

ENGLISH hymnody as we know it today is the result of the confluence of three streams, the nonconformist, led by Isaac Watts, the evangelical revival, typified by Charles Wesley, and the catholic revival through the Oxford Movement, making available the old Greek and Latin traditions, of which the most notable name is John Mason Neale. There are other minor tributaries, such as those coming from Moravian and Lutheran sources. In this book I have offered portrait studies of some of the personalities most involved. I have tried to see these men and women in their setting of life and work, to depict the kind of people they were, and in the light of that to estimate their contribution to hymnody. Some examination of individual hymns is naturally included, but I have deliberately said little about the technicalities of prosody, which appeal only to the few. I have tried to provide human interest without succumbing to the trivial anecdotage which afflicts so many books about hymns; and I have tried to be factual and accurate without presenting the reader with dry lists of names and dates.

As part of my study I have enquired as to the fate today of the hymns of those concerned in the developing history. For this purpose I have taken as my standard their place or absence in the hymn books most used today in British churches: *Hymns Ancient and Modern*, 1950; *The Baptist Hymn Book*, 1962, now on the point of replacing the *Baptist Church Hymnal, Revised*, 1933; *the BBC Hymn Book*, 1951; *The Church Hymnary Revised*, 1927, the Presbyterian book; *Congregational Praise*, 1951; *The English Hymnal*, 1906; *The Methodist Hymn Book*, 1933; *Songs of Praise Enlarged*, 1931. It is these I mean when I refer to the eight current books.

My indebtedness to a host of sources, modern and ancient, is I hope adequately acnowledged in the footnotes. There is inevitably much reference to the monumental and indispensable *Dictionary of Hymnology*, edited by Dr Julian, first published in 1891 and revised in 1907. It is sometimes referred to merely as Julian.

Happily we can use hymns in public worship or private prayer without knowing who wrote them or in what circumstances, but they become much more alive and interesting and spiritually helpful when we know something about the writers and what lies behind them in national or personal history. At least I find it so, and I hope this book will make some of this available to others. My story covers, roughly speaking, the formative period up to the end of the nineteenth century. These hymns are the classics. Happily English hymnody is very much alive, and the last half century has made an appreciable contribution with many interesting features. But I have covered quite enough ground for a modestly sized volume.

HUGH MARTIN

# 1

# SONGS BEFORE UNKNOWN
*The Achievement of Isaac Watts* (1674-1748)

IN his *Journal* for Wednesday, October 4th, 1738, John Wesley has this entry: '1-30 at Dr Watts', conversed. 2-30 walked, singing, conversed.'[1] Here indeed is provoking brevity. His brother Charles was also present. John was 35 and Charles 31, both young, unknown men, only at the beginnings of their astonishing labours. Dr Watts was 64, an outstanding and famous figure. What a meeting! How one wishes to know what John and the Doctor had to say to one another, to have overheard the conversation between the two greatest English hymn writers (though Watts' work in this field was done and that of Wesley hardly begun)—and to know what they sang!

Whether Charles Wesley or Isaac Watts is the greater hymn writer is a much debated question, and it is hard to know by what standard it could be decided. Wesley certainly wrote many more, 6,500 to Watts' 750, and more of his are in common use today, though not so great a proportion of his total output. Wesley has a greater popular appeal. For myself I can only say that Watts speaks for and to my soul as Wesley cannot, and that, profoundly grateful as I am for Wesley's hymns, I count the greatest of Watts' as greater than anything Wesley ever wrote. What is beyond dispute is that Watts started a new era in public worship and that to him 'more than to any other man', as Bernard Manning has written, 'is due the triumph of the hymn in English worship'.

Most of us know Watts only as a hymn writer and there is surprising ignorance about him in quarters where better things might be expected. For he was a quite considerable person even leaving his hymns out of the reckoning, and would deserve a

[1] *John Wesley's Journal*, Edited by N. Curnock, Epworth Press, Vol. II, p. 81.

place in Christian history, and certainly in Free Church history, even if he had written none. As scholar, poet, educational pioneer, preacher, ecclesiastical statesman, he became by his later years a national, and indeed an international, figure. Some of this judgment will, I hope, be sufficiently justified in this chapter. For corroboration I must refer to the biographies, and chiefly to the one by Arthur P. Davis,[1] who has assembled a mass of information, and to the rather less scholarly but more human one by Thomas Wright.[2]

Watts was born in Southampton, of sturdy nonconformist stock. His paternal grandfather died in battle as commander of a warship in what I may call Cromwell's navy. His mother's family were Huguenot in origin. Both families were well-to-do and prominent in the religious and civic life of the town. His father, also Isaac by name, was a clothmaker and, apparently at the same time, head of what a contemporary describes as a 'flourishing boarding school'. When young Isaac was born his father, a deacon in the Above Bar Independent Church, formed at the time of the 1662 expulsion, was in prison along with his minister for his dissenting principles. Indeed he was sent to prison again for six months nine years later, in 1683, and found it wiser after that to live in London apart from his wife and children, to avoid further trouble. So the Watts family had good reason for joining in the rejoicings over the Glorious Revolution of 1688, when William of Orange brought some much needed toleration to dissenters. In later years Isaac junior was to see the final collapse of the ill-fated Stuart regime, in the accession of the House of Hanover and the failure of the rising of 1745. All this is ancient history to us—but it was contemporary to Isaac Watts. To him and to his fellows it meant constitutional monarchy instead of the divine right of kings, a Protestant instead of a Roman Catholic royal house, and—not least—the beginning of religious liberty and equality.

Young Isaac was a promising boy, and a group of Southampton folk offered to send him to Oxford or Cambridge. But as that would have meant joining the Church of England he went

[1] *Isaac Watts*, Independent Press, 1948.
[2] *The Life of Isaac Watts*, Thomas Wright, London, 1914.

instead, at the age of sixteen, to the Dissenting Academy in the country village of Stoke Newington.

Educationally he probably suffered not at all by going to the Academy rather than to one of the universities, though of course their social status was very different. Oxford and Cambridge were then at a very low ebb, perhaps in part owing to the expulsion of all the nonconformist dons and undergraduates, while the Academies had a very high reputation in tone, curriculum and general level of learning. After 1662 nonconformists were debarred from the universities and their enemies did their best to shut them out from all education. The Academies they provided for themselves were often conducted at first by Puritan Fellows and tutors of Oxford and Cambridge who had been ejected. While not neglecting the classics, they led the way in devoting attention to the newer scientific subjects and to modern languages. Among their students were many who attained national and international distinction. They included three archbishops, Secker of Canterbury, Hart of Tuam, and Godwin of Cashel, the famous Bishop Butler of Durham, a Lord Chancellor, Peter King, Daniel Defoe, Isaac Watts, Malthus, Priestley, the scientist, and John Howard, the prison reformer. They had many lay students in addition to the ministerial ones. More than three hundred of their students won a place in the *Dictionary of National Biography*. They made a valuable contribution to the development of English education and deserve to be better known than they are.[1]

After four years at Stoke Newington Watts spent some two years at home before going as tutor to the son of a wealthy dissenter in London. Two years after that he became assistant to Dr Chauncey, the minister of a wealthy and aristocratic Independent Church in Mark Lane in the city of London. In 1702, after much hesitation due to the beginnings of the ill-health which dogged him all his life, he accepted a call to the pastorate. In his first six years the congregation had to move twice to larger premises, but in 1712 he became seriously ill, with fever followed by nervous troubles, including neuralgia. I do not know what

---

[1] I have quoted here from my book, *Puritanism and Richard Baxter*, SCM Press, 1954, pp. 139f. Further information about the Academies may be found in *Dissenting Academies in England*, I. Parker, CUP, 1914, *English Education under the Test Acts*, H. McLachlan, Manchester University Press, 1931, *Studies in English Puritanism*, C. E. Whiting, SPCK, 1931.

name modern medicine would give to his disease, but it certainly led to incapacitating weakness; contemporaries refer to 'violent Jaundice and colic'. Sir Thomas Abney, a wealthy city merchant who was a member of the church, carried him off to convalesce at his country home near Cheshunt, and with the Abneys, as an honoured and beloved member of the family, he was to live for the rest of his life. He remained minister of the church, preaching from time to time but with a co-pastor who carried the main burden.

Watts never married. His small size, five feet, was a constant source of regret to him and seems to have led to his rejection by the woman he loved.[1] She was enchanted by his published poetry and wrote to tell him so and that she longed to meet the poet himself, but she was apparently disillusioned when she did, at least so far as appearances went. They became life-long friends but when he proposed she is reported to have said that though she greatly loved the jewel she could not admire the casket which contained it! Was it then, I wonder, that Isaac burst out with this verse?—

> Were I so tall to reach the Pole,
> Or grasp the ocean with my span,
> I must be measured by my soul;
> The mind's the standard of the man.

For all his small stature he apparently had a fine voice, and certainly was an impressive preacher to congregations that used to contain many of the most learned and distinguished men of his day. He achieved fame and growing influence with both Dissenters and Anglicans as preacher, poet, and writer. In 1728 both Aberdeen and Edinburgh made him a Doctor of Divinity. He had a large correspondence with evangelical circles in Europe and America, and became a man to reckon with in the national life.

Of his poetry and his theology something must be said shortly, but it is important to note that his interests ranged much more widely. He wrote many volumes. His textbook on logic was in use for a hundred years at Oxford and Cambridge, as well as at Harvard and Yale. A work on astronomy was commended by the professionals. *The Improvement of the Mind*, a guide to the best methods of study, had a large and long continued circulation. He

---

[1] Elizabeth Singer, afterwards Mrs Rowe, a noted but very minor poet, of sentimental vein.

had a considerable influence in the educational world, both in the direction of the Academies and in the work of the Charity Schools, the forerunners of our national system, and his educational views were well in advance of his age. Add to all this that he was a talented amateur artist, and you will find it difficult to avoid suspecting that he spread himself too thinly. That was the verdict of Dr Johnson, who admired him greatly as a man and for his learning: 'It would not be safe to claim for him the highest rank in any single denomination of literary dignity, yet perhaps there was nothing in which he would not have excelled if he had not divided his powers to different pursuits'. It is said that hundreds of the definitions in Johnson's famous *Dictionary* are taken from Watts' *Logic*!

But whatever fame Watts may have gathered in his own day in other ways, it is through his hymns that his influence has been most notable and enduring. The story has often been told of how at the age of twenty, on his return from Stoke Newington, he was on his way home from church with his father and complained of the dreary quality of the hymns they had been singing. 'Then give us something better, young man', retorted his father, probably not expecting to be taken seriously. But young Isaac had a hymn ready for the following Sunday morning. The congregation liked it and asked for more, so he went on writing a new hymn for each Sunday for two years until he left home for London. His first hymn began thus:

> Behold the glories of the Lamb
> Amidst His Father's throne.
> Prepare new honours for His name
> And songs before unknown.

'Songs before unknown' were certainly to be forthcoming from this new writer, for though he had predecessors he far surpassed them all. It was to appear as Hymn No. 1 in a volume of *Hymns and Spiritual Songs* thirteen years later.

To understand Watts' discontent and the difficulties to be met we must appreciate the prevailing conditions of public worship. Normally only metrical psalms were sung, in the stilted version of Sternhold and Hopkins or possibly in that of Tate and Brady, which was just a shade better. Many people thought it wrong to sing anything but psalms, but the congregation at Above Bar apparently supplemented them by the hymns of Barton, well-intentioned but heavy going, which had achieved some popularity among Independents in particular. The inability of many to read made necessary the dreadful practice of 'lining'—that is, of reading and singing hymns a line at a time. The leadership was in the hands of a precentor, not always very skilled. Tunes were few and the notes were reduced to 'a constant uniformity of time', long drawn out. The congregation had no words or tune before them and there was no instrumental music. People must often have failed to catch correctly the words given out. Watts complains in the preface of his *Hymns* that much apathy attended such 'singing'. The imagination boggles at what it all must have been like!

Yet with youthful enthusiasm Watts pursued his campaign. His first hymn was written as a youth of twenty in 1694. In 1707, aged 33, he published a volume containing 210 original hymns and twelve doxologies. The classification caters for current opinion. Book I consists of 78 paraphrases, and some people would be willing to sing nothing else. Some, on the authority of Matt. 26.30, were willing to sing a hymn at the Lord's Supper, and Watts provides a section of 22 for that. Those who were prepared to use 'free composures' would find 110 of them in Book II. A revised edition eight years later took advantage of criticisms and added 135 more hymns. In 1719 he continued the good work by the issue of *The Psalms of David Imitated in the Language of the New Testament, and Applied to the Christian State and Worship.*

His books made their way slowly. There was much opposition to the very idea of hymn singing, and the issue sometimes split churches in two. But by the time of his death there had been seven editions of the *Psalms* and sixteen of the *Hymns*. Among Congregationalists and Baptists in particular, Watts eventually ousted all competition, winning an extravagant loyalty not unlike the one-time slavery of Methodism to the hymns of Wesley. After two or three private volumes avowedly supplementary to Watts, the semi-official *Congregational Hymn Book* of 1836, edited by Josiah Conder, offered itself not as an independent book but as a supplement to Watts' Psalms and Hymns. The same thing was true of a volume equally famous among the Baptists, Rippon's *Selection* of 1787. As late as 1849 a *Selection of Hymns for the use of Baptist Congregations*, first published in 1828, is stated to be 'intended as a supplement to Dr Watts' Psalms and Hymns' and was bound up with them. He had a lesser but important in-

## Songs Before Unknown

fluence among Presbyterians, Unitarians and Anglicans and in what Julian's *Dictionary* calls 'the first hymn book prepared for use in the Church of England', John Wesley's Charlestown *Collection,* a third of the total was from Watts.

Although it was published after the *Hymns,* it will be convenient to look at the *Psalms* first. Among the paraphrases in his *Hymns* he included fourteen Psalms and comments in the preface: 'After this manner should I rejoice to see a good part of the Book of Psalms fitted for the use of our churches, and David converted into a Christian. In the first, second and third Psalms especially I have attempted a specimen of what I desire and hope some more capable genius will undertake.' In the Preface to the second edition he says: 'Because I cannot persuade others to attempt this glorious work I have suffered myself to be persuaded to begin it and have through divine goodness already proceeded half way through.' The result appeared in 1719 and included 138 psalms, the others being deliberately omitted. There had been numerous earlier English versions: Watts said he had seen 'above twenty', but these were mostly bad, crude and literal. Their aim, said Watts, was 'to make the Hebrew Psalmist speak only English and keep all his own characters (i.e. characteristics) still'. He mentions with special approval the work of Dr John Patrick who had published in 1679 a *Century of Select Psalms and Portions of the Psalms of David, especially those of Praise, for the use of the Charterhouse,* where he was Preacher. Watts praised him particularly as ready to paraphrase and adapt the psalms in a Christian sense, and said he was going to try to carry on from Patrick and to improve on him. Indeed he frequently quotes from Patrick in his own versions, as he acknowledged in his first edition.[1]

'My own design in short is this,' wrote Watts, 'to accommodate the Book of Psalms to Christian worship.' This inevitably meant both selection and adaptation. Many psalms were unChristian in

---

[1] Julian lists 118 'complete or partial versions' of the psalms in English up to the date of Watts' book. For Patrick see Benson, *The English Hymn,* p. 54. Elizabeth's Injunction permitting the singing of a 'hymn' at the beginning of common prayer was a concession to those who wanted metrical as against chanted psalms. The poets and would-be poets of her reign competed in versifying the psalms, and the composers in setting them to music.

sentiment, remote from the conditions of eighteenth century life, and in the nature of things did not contain the characteristic tenets of Christianity. In his own words in the preface to the *Hymns*: 'Some of them are almost opposite to the spirit of the Gospel, many of them are foreign to the state of the New Testament, and widely different from the present circumstances of Christians.'

His preface to the *Psalms of David Imitated* is a vigorous defence of what he is doing, and indeed an attack carrying the war into the enemy's country. He asserts his sense of the incomparable value of the Jewish psalms, but declares that they are not always fit for Christian worship. David, he declares, must be taught 'to speak like a Christian'. Those who still use the psalms in worship with little deletion and no revision, with much consequent irritation, bewilderment and misunderstanding in their congregation, would find it well worth while to ponder his words. Watts entirely omitted several psalms and large pieces of many others, and chose 'such parts only as might easily and naturally be accommodated to the various occasions of the Christian life.' 'I have chosen rather to imitate than to translate: and thus to compose a psalm book for Christians after the manner of the Jewish psalter.' He had expressed himself 'as I may suppose David would have done had he lived in the days of Christianity'.

Watts tried also to relate it all to contemporary English life, sometimes with rather odd results. It is no doubt all right to substitute 'Britain' for 'Israel', but one cannot help being a little surprised when David enters the field of politics and hails 'the glorious Revolution by King William':

> No vain pretence to royal birth
>   Shall fix a tyrant on the throne.
> God, the great Sovereign of the earth,
>   Will rise and make His justice known.

While this particular verse would no doubt have been approved, some of the appearances of David as a patriotic Englishman created difficulties in the use of the book in America after Independence, and made revisions necessary.[1]

Watts spent nineteen years on the job. Some of his versions are poor and few are suitable for use today, but as a whole they were an immense improvement on their predecessors and rendered a

---

[1]See Benson, op. cit., p. 146.

great service. Among them are some of his best known hymns, such as 'Jesus shall reign' and the incomparable 'Our God our help'. Just to compare its familiar lines with the versions of the 90th Psalm which it replaced is to learn something of our debt. Here is Watts:

> A thousand ages in Thy sight
> Are like an evening gone,
> Short as the watch that ends the night
> Before the rising sun.

Here is Sternhold and Hopkins on the same theme:

> The lasting of a thousand years,
> What is it in Thy sight?
> As yesterday it doth appear
> Or as a watch by night.

The 'Old Version' of Sternhold and Hopkins and the 'New Version' of Tate and Brady still counted as Holy Writ with many, and the struggle to replace them was slow and stern. Nevertheless, seven editions of Watts were sold in ten years.

Christians, however, needed hymns of their own: it was not enough to adapt or imitate the psalms. 'Why must we under the Gospel sing nothing else but the joys and hopes and fears of Asaph and David?' It was a relevant question when Watts asked it in the Preface to his *Hymns*. It is true that, in hymns as well as in psalms, he had predecessors, who ought not to be forgotten. Behind him were, for example, the devotional verses of Herbert and Crashaw, not meant for use in church, and those of George Wither, in the days of James I, who would like them to have been so used. His *Hymns and Songs of the Church,* published in 1623, was perhaps the first book of hymns in English.[1] It was intended for use in public worship. But Wither roused opposition in the Company of Stationers by getting a patent from the king that the book should be bound up with every copy of the metrical Psalter. The Stationers put every possible obstacle in the way and eventually secured the cancellation of the patent, continuing even after that to hamper its circulation. There was the pioneer work of Crossman, who was ejected in 1662 but soon conformed and

---

[1] T. C. Crippen in *Encyclopedia of Religion and Ethics*, VII, p. 33, gives this place to Coverdale's *Goostly Psalmes and Spiritual Songs*, 1539, containing 41 hymns, all but five translations from the German. But Wither was the first of any real note.

became Dean of Bristol, the author of the moving hymn, 'My song is love unknown'. John Austin, who became a Roman Catholic, wrote lovely poems, including the hymn for springtime, 'Look, my soul, how everything'. There was Bishop Ken, and Richard Baxter, who did much to encourage others as well as writing himself. One of his friends was John Mason, rector of Water-Stratford, who published his *Spiritual Songs* in 1683, which circulated fairly widely among nonconformists: it was in its eighth edition when Watts issued his own volume. Two fine hymns of his are one for evening, 'Now from the altar of my heart', and 'Thou wast, O God, and Thou wast blest'. Two others of his hymns are in *Congregational Praise*. To the hymns of Barton some reference has already been made. Watts also gained from the courageous efforts of Keach and Stennett among the Baptists in getting hymns used regularly in congregational worship. Their own writings were undistinguished but Watts was probably influenced by their plainness of speech for simple folk, unlike most of the verse of their day. But in spite of the acknowledged debt of Watts to such men, he was still a pioneer and the opposition to singing hymns at all was little placated. Watts had 'a combination of resources, spiritual, intellectual, poetic, utilitarian, possessed by none of his predecessors or all of them if put together'.[1] And he had a better appreciation than they had of the practical possibilities of the situation. He knew the limitations within which he must work if he was to achieve results. He was trying as a working minister to meet the actual needs of congregations as he knew them.

Watts detested the practice of 'lining' but recognized that it was then inevitable. He chafed against the 'fetters' of 'the old narrow metres', long, short and common measure, but knew that these were what congregations were used to, and that even for these they had few tunes. Some managed with only three. Perhaps like too many ministers Watts underestimated the intelligence of his congregations, but he felt it necessary to use the simplest language and the most obvious metaphors in his hymns. He 'endeavoured to make the sense plain and obvious'. 'The metaphors are generally sunk to the level of vulgar capacities. If the verse appears so gentle and flowing as to merit the censure of feebleness I may honestly affirm that it

---

[1] Benson, op. cit., p. 206.

## Songs Before Unknown

sometimes cost me labour to make it so. Some of the beauties of poesy are neglected and some wilfully defaced, lest a more exalted turn of thought or language should darken or disturb the devotions of the weakest souls.'

It has not always been recognized how much both the literary and the spiritual tendencies of his age were against him. John Ellerton, himself one of our best hymn writers, expresses this forcefully: 'The true hymnody of England begins in the much abused eighteenth century, the age whose poetry was prose, as the prose of the seventeenth had been poetry; the age of scepticism in religion, frivolity in taste, laxity in morals; the age of evidences, not of convictions; of toleration not of enthusiasm; an age which sentimentalists think a dead level of dulness; when the devout Churchman had become a tiresome formalist and the brave and earnest Puritan a prudent and prosperous Dissenter. Then it was that, from the pleasant arbour of Sir Thomas Abney's suburban villa, his invalid guest, the gentle nonconformist minister, sent forth at intervals the first really congregational hymns which had appeared since the reign of Elizabeth.'[1]

In saying that he had to curb his poetic powers to suit his purpose, Watts was not boasting. The year before his *Hymns* appeared he had published a volume of poetry, *Horae Lyricae*. The preface revealed a wide knowledge of English poetry and its techniques, while the poems, mostly of a moral or religious trend, included translations from French and Latin, funeral odes and political verse. Other volumes of poetry came later. Though not in the same rank as a poet as Herbert and Cowper, Watts is of the same school. In subject matter and style he was naturally a son of his age, but he was a poet among its poets and deserves his monument in the Poets Corner of Westminster Abbey.

Johnson, who included Watts in his *Lives of the Poets*, wrote: 'Had he been only a poet, he would probably have stood high among the authors with whom he is now associated.' Palgrave passes much the same judgment, and it is valuable as coming from the editor of the famous *Golden Treasury* and Professor of Poetry at Oxford. Watts, he says, sacrificed 'honours in literature' which he had the gifts to attain in order to serve the Church. Cowper, in a letter to John Newton (September 18th, 1781) describes Watts as 'a man of true poetical ability . . . frequently

---

[1] *Life* by Henry Housman, SPCK, 1896, pp. 199f.

sublime in his conceptions and masterly in his execution'. Sampson in *A Century of Divine Song* comments on his use of 'unforgettable epithets' like

> Our everlasting hopes arise
> Above these ruinable skies.

And Saintsbury, no mean judge in such matters, is impressed by the 'prosodic versatility' shown by Watts, and his mastery of poetic forms. Particularly interesting is the opinion of A. E. Housman, himself a poet of no mean distinction but no friend to religious verse, who points to Watts as one of the true poets of the eighteenth century, and quotes the lines from his 'Cradle Hymn':

> Soft and easy is thy cradle,
> Coarse and hard thy Saviour lay,
> When His birthplace was a stable
> And His softest bed was hay.

'This simple verse, bad rhyme and all, is poetry beyond Pope's.'[1] So those of us who reckon Watts among the poets are in good company.

Watts has been unreasonably praised and, no doubt in consequence, has been in some quarters unreasonably depreciated. It is easy enough to criticize and even to make fun of him if you pick the right bits and ignore the rest. Much that he wrote is best forgotten. His theology was not ours and his language was that of the eighteenth century. His verse for children seemed comical to Lewis Carroll in his delightful parodies, just as the language of Carroll's Alice seems amusingly prim and Victorian to today's children. We don't grudge Carroll his laugh, and I for one laugh with him. But that is not to say the last word about Watts, or even about his children's verses.

*Divine Songs, Attempted in Easy Language for the Use of Children* was published in 1715 and went through no fewer than ninety-five editions by 1810. For nearly two centuries it was a nursery classic. Watts said he had been urged to write for children and was very hesitant, but hoped his attempts would provoke somebody else to do better. The verses were tried out on Lady Abney's three little daughters in the family circle. The moral sometimes seems dragged in—as in some modern children's addresses. There are some dreadful verses of gloomy and doubtful theology: one can only hope that they slid harmlessly over

[1] *The Name and Nature of Poetry*, p. 30.

the heads of the children, as no doubt they did. There are signs too of a long prevalent desire, not entirely dead yet, to frighten children into being good. But the book as a whole is not like that at all and is mostly gentle, persuasive and quietly humorous—a gift which some of his critics seem to lack—and deeply Christian. In spite of all its defects it was much the best thing of its kind available. Benson, one of our greatest hymnologists, hails it as 'the fountainhead of the afterwards extensive children's hymnody in the English language'.[1]

How many know that *Divine Songs* is the source of many sayings that have become almost proverbial?

>How doth the little busy bee
>   Improve each shining hour,
>And gather honey all the day
>   From every opening flower!

And >Satan finds some mischief still
>   For idle hands to do.

And >Let dogs delight to bark and bite,
>   For God hath made them so.

The pick of its contents is the lovely 'Cradle Hymn' already quoted, which George Sampson says is 'worthy of Blake himself, who was not to be born till over forty years later.' Here also is 'I sing the almighty power of God', still one of the best of children's hymns.

It is interesting to know that Watts published a graded Catechism, arranged for children of 4 to 5; 8 to 9; 10 to 12. In so realizing the need for grading he was well ahead of his time. And what a tribute to his versatility! 'Every man acquainted with the common principles of human action,' wrote Dr Johnson in his ponderous way, 'will look with veneration on the writer who is at one time combating Locke and at another making a catechism for children in their fourth year.'

In his hymns generally Watts is frequently guilty of bad rhymes. He will match 'sin' with 'divine' and 'clean'; 'dumb' with 'room'; 'suns' with 'once'; even, as we have seen, try to get away with 'cradle' as a rhyme for 'stable'. The worst crime that I have detected is the rhyming of 'see it' with 'feet'. Some of his, to us, bad rhymes were common practice in his day and can be found in Pope. Some are excused by the fact that the pronunciation has

[1]Op. cit. p. 127.

changed: the eighteenth century, for example, pronounced 'toil' to rhyme with 'isle,' 'sea,' like 'tea', did rhyme with 'away', and 'lamb' and 'name' sounded the same. But when all is said many must be put down to plain carelessness. And he uses some funny words, like 'bowels' and 'worms' in the most incongruous contexts. One must remember that much that strikes us as odd was perfectly normal when he wrote.

But then poor verses and feeble rhymes can be found easily enough in the works of many a much greater poet, like Wordsworth or Tennyson. We must not lose our sense of proportion so far as to forget the immense debt we owe to young Isaac Watts, with his enthusiasm, his poetic craftsmanship, and his readiness to blaze a trail through little explored country. Soon no one would produce a book of hymns without protesting that he had no intention of competing with Dr Watts, and after the winnowing of some two centuries some of them are still among our greatest treasures. I like the letter that Doddridge, a faithful disciple, addressed to Watts towards the end of his long life. 'Above all I congratulate you that by your sacred poetry, especially by your Psalms and your Hymns, you are leading the worship and I trust also animating the devotions of myriads in our public assemblies every Sabbath, and in their families and closets every day. This, sir, at least so far as it relates to the service of the sanctuary is an unparalleled favour by which God hath been pleased to distinguish you, I may boldly say it, beyond any of His servants now upon earth.'[1]

Let me try to set down the characteristic emphasis of his hymns as I see them.

1. First of all is his emphasis on the sovereignty and majesty of God, as in those familiar lines in what Sampson has called 'the greatest of all English hymns'[2]:

> Before the hills in order stood,
>   Or earth received her frame,
> From everlasting Thou art God,
>   To endless years the same.

---

[1]Gibbons, *Memoirs of the Rev Isaac Watts, D.D.*, London, 1700, p. 306, Letter of 13th December, 1744.
[2]*A Century of Divine Song*, p. 6.

## Songs Before Unknown

Or less familiar:

> Still restless nature dies and grows,
>   From change to change the creatures run,
> Thy being no succession knows
>   And all Thy vast designs are one.
>
> Who can behold the blazing light?
>   Who can approach consuming flame?
> None but Thy wisdom knows Thy might,
>   None but Thy word can speak Thy name.

Watts, Doddridge, Montgomery, Newton, Bonar, who appear in this book as among the great makers of English hymnody, might all be described as 'liberal Calvinists', though that expression was probably unknown to them. They were not of the extreme kind, which did exist. But, like Calvin himself, they found their Gospel, their strength and their inspiration in an overwhelming sense of the sovereign majesty and redeeming grace of God. That is the soul and heart of Calvinism, not speculations about the nature of predestination, which is unhappily all that some people seem to see in it.

2. Watts has much to say about the transiency and unsatisfactoriness of earthly life. He saw 'the tears in things', as all the great poets have done. He looked at the fact of human sin squarely and with no false sentimentality. He could not forget the solemn issues of life or the frailty of human goodness. This note is rather played down in the selections in contemporary hymn books.

3. But 'though there is much so-called calvinistic gloom in his poetry there is also much more evangelical hope.'[1] He radiates joy and praise. As Julian says, there is 'a pervading cheerfulness and buoyant faith'. Indeed joy and cheerfulness are among his most characteristic words, and how welcome is his claim that

> Religion never was designed
>   To make our pleasures less.

'Come,' he cries,

> Come, let us join our cheerful songs
>   With angels round the throne.

Or

> Come, we that love the Lord
>   And let our joys be known.
>
> Let those refuse to sing
>   That never knew our God,

---

[1] Davis, op. cit., p. 163.

> But children of the heavenly King
> Must speak their joys abroad.

And in the same hymn he tells us that when we reach 'the fairer worlds on high' we shall 'drink endless pleasures in' from 'the rivers of His grace'.

4. All his thought is Christ-centred. One thinks of such hymns as 'Join all the glorious names', 'With joy we meditate the grace', and 'When I survey the wondrous cross'.[1] Watts was much involved in controversy about the doctrine of the Trinity, and wrote several books trying to produce a tidy, logical and philosophical explanation—which no man can do, and which is the wrong method of approach. Seeking to reconcile opposing parties, he was abused by both, as often happens, and was accused by the orthodox of being himself a Unitarian. He certainly never regarded himself as one and his hymns are sufficient answer to the charge. When Unitarians use them they have to chop the heart out of them.

> Almighty God to Thee
> Be endless honours done,
> The undivided Three
> And mysterious One.
> Where reason fails with all her powers
> There faith prevails and love adores.

The man who could write that was no Unitarian.

5. To Watts the Christian faith is an affair of cosmic and not only of earthly significance, and he calls on all nature to join him in his worship. Bernard Manning refers to 'a sense of the spaciousness of nature, of the vastness of time, of the dreadfulness of eternity, in Watts which is missing or less felt in Wesley',[2] which is perhaps part of the same thing.

> Ere the blue heavens were stretched abroad
> From everlasting was the Word.

And at the centre of all, astounding paradox, is a crucified Creator! 'Jesus the God, was born to die.'

> Well might the sun in darkness hide
> And shut his glories in

---

[1] Others that might be quoted in this connection are 'Nature with open volume stands', 'Now to the Lord a noble song', 'I'm not ashamed to own my Lord'.

[2] *The Hymns of Wesley and Watts*, Epworth Press, 1942, p. 83.

## Songs Before Unknown

> When God, the mighty Maker, died
> For man, the creature's sin.

Elsewhere he writes

> Our souls adore th' eternal God
> Who condescended to be born.

It is the wonder of 'love so amazing, so divine', that makes him sing

> Let all that dwell above the sky
> And air and earth and seas
> Conspire to lift Thy glories high
> And speak Thy endless praise.
>
> The whole creation join in one
> To bless the sacred name
> Of Him that sits upon the throne
> And to adore the Lamb.

6. His missionary outlook, long before the days of the missionary societies, is noteworthy. As illustration note how he introduces into his version of Psalm 19 a thought that is not there at all.

> Nor shall Thy spreading Gospel rest
> Till through the earth Thy truth has run,
> Till Christ has all the nations blest
> That see the light or feel the sun.

And one of the best of our missionary hymns comes from Watts, 'Jesus shall reign'. Two admirable verses of this are usually omitted:

> Behold the islands with their kings,
> And Europe her best tribute brings,
> From north to south the princes meet
> To pay their homage at His feet.
>
> There Persia, glorious to behold,
> There India, shines in eastern gold;
> And barbarous nations at His word
> Submit and bow and own their Lord.

I like his quaint summing up:

> What though we go the world around
> And search from Britain to Japan,
> There shall be no religion found
> So just to God, so safe for man.

7. Outstanding also is the surpassing quality of thought, depth

of feeling and beauty of language in his hymns about the future life. I am thinking of 'There is a land of pure delight', 'Give me the wings of faith', and 'How bright those glorious spirits shine'.

8. Lastly, Watts book contained a special section of twenty-two Communion hymns, among them 'When I survey the wondrous cross'. Anglican theologians have been known to accuse us in the Free Churches of regarding the Lord's Supper as 'a mere memorial' of the past and of having no true notion of the nature of a sacrament. When they do that in my hearing I tell them that a complete answer could be found by looking at any of our hymn books. It would be enough only to look at the hymns of Isaac Watts.

> Jesus invites His saints
> To meet around His board
> Where pardoned rebels sit and hold
> Communion with their Lord.[1]

It is not strange that owing to differences in theological outlook, changing language, a new social setting, improved popular education, many of Watts' hymns should have fallen into disuse. Rightly and inevitably, Watts belonged to his own time. What I find impressive is the number of his hymns that still survive and serve in our vastly different world. Indeed the tendency in the most recent hymn books is for the number of his hymns to increase. Perhaps twenty-five to thirty are in general use, while *Congregational Praise* includes as many as forty-eight.

Watts is, beyond dispute, 'the father of English hymnody', in Lord Selborne's words, and his writings still compete with their distant descendants. And I have yet to meet a modern hymn that surpasses 'When I survey the wondrous Cross' or 'Our God, our help in ages past'.

---

[1] His own word 'rebels' is surely more colourful and impressive than 'sinners' which *Congregational Praise* has substituted.

# 2

## HARK THE GLAD SOUND!

*Philip Doddridge's hymns to 'fix' the sermon*
(1702-1751)

TOWARDS the end of his life Isaac Watts paid a remarkable tribute to his friend Philip Doddridge. He was writing to David Longueville, the minister of the English Church in Amsterdam. 'I have no need to give you a large account of his knowledge in the sciences, in which I confess him to be greatly my superior. . . . He hath a most skilful and condescending way of instruction, nor is there any person of my acquaintance with whom I am more entirely agreed in all the sentiments of the doctrine of Christ. . . . Since I am now advanced in age beyond my seventieth year, if there were any man to whom Providence would permit me to commit a second part of my life and usefulness in the Church of Christ, Dr Doddridge should be the man.'[1]

Certainly Doddridge on his side was a devoted admirer and disciple of the older man. In the preface to his most famous book, *The Rise and Progress of Religion in the Soul*, he wrote at length of the debt that he and the whole Christian world owed to Watts for his varied and outstanding services. The book itself had been projected by Watts who had been forced by illness to hand over its writing to Doddridge. Watts was deeply involved in the work of the Nonconformist Academies and had helped in getting Doddridge appointed as principal of one of them and in securing funds for its maintenance. As a hymn writer Doddridge was a conscious follower. Both men had a family tradition of persecution for conscience sake. Both had been offered university education if they would give up their nonconformity. Both were eirenic, 'ecumenical' spirits. Both rendered astonishing service to the Christian cause in spite of life-long physical weakness.

Doddridge was born in London, where his father was in busi-

[1]Gibbons, op. cit., p. 309.

ness as an 'oil man', on June 26th, 1702. Out of twenty children only he and a sister lived to maturity. Indeed it was only because a keen-eyed servant noted a flicker of life in the new-born infant that Philip himself survived. As a child his mother told him Bible stories with the aid of the pictures on the Dutch tiles in the fireplace. He heard too of how her father had fled in disguise from Prague as a refugee with, for all his possessions, the clothes he wore, some money stitched into his leather belt and his copy of Luther's Bible. If he could have forgotten such a thrilling story, the treasured Bible was there to remind him. Stirring too was the story of how his other grandfather, John Doddridge, with his ten children, had left his comfortable vicarage after the 1662 Act of Uniformity, to throw in his lot with the nonconformists.[1] Perhaps he heard of another ancestor who had been a Judge of the King's Bench in the reign of James I and of the family estates in Devon that had once been theirs.

At the age of ten he was sent to the old Grammar School at Kingston-on-Thames, apparently not the one where his grandfather Baumann had taught. Three years later his father died and, soon after, his mother. 'I am under peculiar obligation,' he said years later in a sermon, 'to desire and attempt the relief of orphans, as I know the heart of an orphan.' A certain Mr Downes of St Albans, a kindly but feckless creature, became his guardian, but by 1717 had lost all Philip's property as well as his own by foolish speculation. Doddridge had to leave school and his future was precarious indeed. His uncle Philip was steward to the Bedford estates, and he had often spent his holidays there, playing with the Russell children and becoming something of a pet of the Duchess. When she heard of his plight she generously offered to send him at her own expense to the university with the promise of an Anglican living later. But Doddridge, like Watts before him, clung to nonconformity. He appealed for advice and help to Dr Edmund Calamy, one of the outstanding dissenting ministers of the day, but he discouraged him from training for

---

[1] According to the Parliamentary Survey of 1650 the living had a yearly income of £130, with glebe land of nineteen acres and the tithes of a number of farms. Allowing for the changed value of money, all this must have amounted to a considerable sum. John Doddridge became vicar of Shepperton in 1649. After 1662 he became pastor of a small dissenting congregation near Brentford. See *Philip Doddridge*, Charles Stanford, Hodder and Stoughton, 1880.

the ministry, perhaps because of his youth and his poor health. In his distress a letter arrived from his old pastor in St Albans, Dr Samuel Clark, offering him a home and promising to see him through his ministerial training. It was like 'an answer from heaven', Philip wrote in his diary. So in December, 1719, he entered the Dissenting Academy at Kibworth and later at Hinckley, presided over by John Jennings, in whom he found an inspiring teacher.

In 1723 Doddridge became minister at Kibworth to a congregation of some 150 humble folk. This allowed him leisure for study which he grasped to the full, laying further foundations for his learning and his astonishing knowledge of books. In July, 1729, at the request of a group of ministers, he himself started an Academy, in conjunction with his pastorate, at Market Harborough. He had declined several flattering invitations to larger churches, partly because he suspected them of a narrow theological outlook with which he would not have been at home. But later the same year he accepted a call to the pastorate of Castle Hill Independent Church, Northampton, and moved there with his Academy. The church had 342 members: at the end of his ministry it had 239. This was partly due to a number being drawn away by a very eccentric Moravian meeting started near by. But, allowing for that, the numbers are a good guide to the difficult conditions under which his work had to be done. Not only Doddridge but many of his contemporaries had cause to lament what it was usual to call 'the decline of the dissenting interest'. In many of the churches there was 'great lukewarmness and indifference', a lack of vitality. The growth of unitarianism had lessened their zeal and evangelistic spirit.

Before long Doddridge had to face a serious attack on his Academy. A law of 1603 said that no man could be master in a grammar school without a licence from the bishop of the diocese, and an attempt was made to revive this in order to crush the nonconformist academies. Northampton was to be a test case, and a summons was issued in 1732. Doddridge refused to apply for a licence and sought help from the recently formed Dissenting Deputies. Made up of two representatives of each nonconformist church in London they united Baptists, Independents and Presbyterians in a very necessary defence of their civil rights, and played a most valuable part for some two hundred years in the defence and extension of religious liberty in this country. Realizing the importance of the issue, they took the case as far as the highest court of appeal at Westminster Hall. The prolonged argument there was put a stop to by the personal intervention of George II, who had set his face against any form of religious persecution.

Job Orton, his pupil, assistant, biographer, and editor of his hymns, speaks of the affection with which Doddridge was regarded by his students and of his personal influence on them, though he was no disciplinarian. On average he had thirty-four students. During the twenty-two years of his headship some two hundred in all went through his hands. His rather formal, scholastic, logical method of lecturing came in for some criticism, and even more his habit of stating the arguments for and against any particular view with references to writers on both sides. He left it too much to his students to make up their own minds, and did not give them enough positive lead: so it was said. But his intellectual ability and wide learning were unchallenged. The fact that he was consulted by Wesley as to a course of reading for young ministers is some testimony to his great knowledge of books.

In addition to his pastorate and his college, he took a great interest in social and political questions. He worked for the prisoners in the county jail. He established a charity school for the clothing and teaching of twenty boys. He was concerned for the widows and orphans of ministers. He was active in promoting, in the face of much popular opposition, the practice of inoculation against the scourge of smallpox. Most memorable in this connection, perhaps, was the leading part he took in the foundation of the Northampton County Infirmary, the first of its kind. The 1745 Stuart rising also brought him to the fore. The Dissenters were still smarting from the wrongs done to them under the Stuarts in civil disabilities, fines and imprisonments, and general denial of spiritual liberty. Moreover the Stuarts in exile were avowed Roman Catholics and pensioners of France. The Georges were not personally popular, but the Dissenters generally ardently supported them because of what they represented, as constitutional, Protestant monarchs. Many in the country generally would, however, have welcomed a restoration of the Stuarts, and there was a great deal of apathy in England about the outcome when Charles Edward landed in Scotland. Not till he set out for London with his army of Highlanders was anything serious done to raise the necessary troops to resist him. Doddridge had been active in helping to raise a Northamptonshire

## Hark The Glad Sound!

regiment under the Earl of Halifax. He corresponded with the Secretary of State in London and rallied nonconformity to the support of the government.

Being the man he was, it is not surprising that he had a host of correspondents and much of his time was taken up in writing letters.[1] It is in this correspondence that his real self can be seen, rather than in Orton's biography or in his formal writings. Playful and witty as well as deeply serious and sympathetic, there are some of them not unworthy to be mentioned in the same sentence as the immortal letters of William Cowper.

He was one of the first among nonconformists to follow Richard Baxter in an ardent concern for foreign missions. The needs of the American Indians particularly appealed to him. He started a missionary auxiliary in his own church and tried to secure volunteers among his students for missionary work.[2] There is a moving story of how a party of Indians, accompanied by a missionary, arrived in a town in Pennsylvania on their way to Philadelphia at the invitation of President and Congress. Local folk gave them a welcome and at a meeting in the church hymns were sung in English, which some of them understood. 'After a short pause a select company of them rose and joined their minister in singing hymns in the same strain in the Indian language, among which was that beautiful hymn of Dr Doddridge, "Jesus, I love Thy charming name".' How Doddridge would have rejoiced at that! He had the stimulus in his missionary interest of contacts with the Moravians, including a personal meeting with Zinzendorf in 1741, and became a supporter of their English society. Subsequent events unfortunately produced some disillusionment, as they did with Watts and Wesley.

And all the while he was writing books, fifty-three of them, large and small, some in several volumes and some only pamphlets. He is said to have worked at his *Family Expositor* for fifteen years before he published the first of its six volumes in 1739. Over many years it had a large circulation and a wide influence. *The Rise and Progress of Religion in the Soul*, already

---

[1] His *Correspondence and Diary* was published in no less than five volumes in 1829-31.

[2] His missionary enthusiasm, fifty years before the creation of the great missionary societies, is admirably summarized by Dr E. A. Payne in the volume on *Philip Doddridge*, edited by G. F. Nuttall, Independent Press, 1951.

mentioned, is an earnest, impressive work, but with few literary graces and a rather heavy, laboured style. The modern reader may wonder at the immense influence it exerted for many years among wise and simple. It does not make easy reading today. His books sold by the hundred thousand and editions appeared in America and translations in France, Holland, Germany, Denmark and Wales. Aberdeen made him a Doctor of Divinity in 1736.

Doddridge was an eager promoter of friendly relations between all the churches. His vestry was always available when the College Lane Baptist Church wished to hold a baptismal service in the nearby river Nene, as their custom then was, and Doddridge frequently spoke in their church. He was much criticized for his support of the Wesleys and Whitefield, when nonconformists generally, including Watts who sternly reproved him, looked askance at their revivalist methods. He invited John Wesley to address his students and allowed Whitefield to occupy his pulpit. He managed to be friends with Wesley, Whitefield and the Countess of Huntingdon, who were seldom friendly with one another. He was on terms of close friendship with several heads of colleges at Oxford and Cambridge, and with many leading Anglicans. In consequence he was accused of compromising his principles and being a poor sort of nonconformist. To one such critic he wrote in 1748: 'Though my growing acquaintance with many excellent persons, some of them of great eminence, in the Establishment, increases those candid, respectful sentiments of that body of Christians which I had long entertained; yet I am so thoroughly persuaded of the reasonableness of nonconformity and find so many of the terms of ministerial conformity contrary to the dictates of my conscience in the sight of God, that I was never less inclined to submit to them, and hope I shall not be willing to buy my liberty or life at that price. But I think it is my duty to do my part towards promoting that mutual peace and goodwill that I think more likely than anything else either to reform the Church, or else to promote true Christianity both in the Establishment and separation.'

What with all this—his church, his college, his writing, his correspondence, and his care of all the churches—it is not surprising to find the *Dictionary of National Biography* suggesting that Doddridge had too many irons in the fire, or to discover that he was criticized for inadequate preparation of his sermons. He

## Hark The Glad Sound! 33

is described by those who knew him as a kindly, courteous, happy tempered man, almost over anxious to be fair to those with whom he disagreed. Dr Nuttall quotes a friend of Doddridge as saying that 'he never knew a man of so gay a temper.'[1] His private papers and letters reveal a deep, disciplined spiritual life. He was most happily married to Mercy Maris. Five of their nine children died in infancy. The appalling infant mortality of those days, sufficiently illustrated by the Doddridge family alone, must still distress anyone who brings imagination to his historical reading.

He acquired an immense reputation and influence far beyond the bounds of his own denomination or even his own country, which lived long after him. When Stoughton wrote his centenary tribute he recorded that his influence was undiminished through his books and his hymns, and that his *Life of Colonel Gardiner* and his *Rise and Progress* were still in circulation. With his frail physique the extent of his work was astonishing, but he was still in his forties when his friends watched with deep concern his tall, slender, stooping form, his thin flushed features, the hurried breath and the hollow cough. Holidays in England did no good, and a group of friends put together the money to send him to Lisbon to winter in a milder climate. He preached his last sermon in Northampton on July 1st, 1751. He died in Lisbon on October 26th.

Doddridge's hymns were for the most part written to be sung after his sermons at Castle Hill, 'lined out' by the precentor. They were collected after his death and transcribed from the original shorthand by his friend, Job Orton, as *Hymns founded on various texts in the Holy Scriptures by the late Philip Doddridge, D.D. Salop*, 1755. They were often reprinted and were used in some churches as a supplement to Watts. In 1839 another edition appeared, edited by his great grandson, John Doddridge Humphreys, described as 'a new and corrected edition, containing many hymns never before printed, edited from the original documents'. Humphreys declared that Orton had performed his task in an 'extraordinarily incorrect and unsatisfactory manner'. He had made errors in transcribing the shorthand, which Orton confessed sometimes defeated him, and put his own words in to fill up gaps he could not read. Modern editors, for some reason, usually

[1]Op. cit., p. 154.

follow Orton, but my vote, where they vary, is for Humphreys. There are also two additional manuscript collections noted by Julian. Humphreys' edition is arranged according to the biblical origins of the texts, which prove to be almost equally divided between the Old and the New Testaments: 397 hymns, 194 based on Old Testament texts.

Orton writes in his preface: 'These Hymns being composed to be sung when the Author had been preaching on the texts prefixed to them, it was his Design that they should bring over again the leading Thoughts in the Sermon and naturally express and warmly enforce those devout Sentiments, which he hoped were then rising in the Minds of his Hearers and help to fix them on the Memory and Heart.' Being thus attached firmly to the sermon and written in the glow of its composition, they were often written hastily and without polishing or any thought of publication. They were sung when the sermon was fresh in the minds of the congregation: many indeed are so much an echo of it that they are really unintelligible without it. Comparatively few are of any general or permanent value. Julian says that seventy of them were in common use in 1892, but no current hymnal has more than fourteen.[1] This is a small harvest, but those that do survive are of great value and his place in English hymnody is an important one.

Several are straightforward paraphrases and three of them appear in amended form among the *Scottish Paraphrases*. Most are naturally expositions, following no doubt the line of the sermon. There are a number of ordination hymns, probably written for use when his students were being ordained. Some are for use at the opening of a new place of worship, doubtless when Doddridge was the special preacher. One is headed 'On the occasion of a dreadful fire' and one concerns a plague among cattle. There are numerous national hymns, and one is worth quoting for its interesting combination of references. It is headed 'A Song for the Fifth of November. God's delivering goodness acknowledged and trusted. II Cor. 1,10.' It will be seen that it

---

[1] *Congregational Praise* has 14; *Baptist Hymn Book* 8; *Methodist Hymn Book* 7; *BBC* and *Church Hymnary* both 6; *Ancient and Modern*, 1950, 5; *English Hymnal* 4 and *Songs of Praise* 3. Most of these may fairly be thought to undervalue him, but *Congregational Praise* retains quite as many as are really usable. Between them the books use 18 of his hymns.

*Hark The Glad Sound!*

covers not only Gunpowder Plot, but the defeat of the Armada, and the 'glorious revolution' of 1688.

> Praise to the Lord, whose mighty hand
> So oft revealed hath saved our land;
> And when united nations rose
> Hath shamed and scourged our haughtiest foes.
>
> When mighty navies from afar
> To Britain wafted floating war,
> His breath dispersed them all with ease
> And sank their terrors in the seas.
>
> While for our princes they prepare
> In caverns deep a burning snare,
> He shot from heaven a piercing ray
> And the dark treachery brought to day.
>
> Princes and priests again combine
> New chains to forge, new snares to twine;
> Again our gracious God appears
> And breaks their chains and cuts their snares.
>
> Obedient winds at His command
> Convey His hero to our land.
> The sons of Rome with terror view
> And speed their flight, when none pursue.
>
> Such great deliverance God hath wrought
> And down to us salvation brought,
> And still the care of guardian Heaven
> Secures the bliss itself hath given.
>
> In Thee we trust, Almighty Lord,
> Continued rescue to afford;
> Still be Thy powerful arm made bare
> For all Thy servants' hopes are there.

The social concern so manifest in his life and somewhat unusual in that day, comes out in a number of his hymns. There is the familiar verse in 'Hark the glad sound', 'He comes the broken heart to heal', but that might be dismissed as paraphrase. Better evidence is in his hymn on the Good Samaritan, not in any of our modern books.

> Father of mercies, send Thy grace
>   All powerful from above,
> To form in our obedient souls
>   The image of Thy love.

> O may our sympathizing breasts
> That generous pleasure know,
> Kindly to share in others' joy
> And weep for others' woe.
>
> When the poor helpless sons of grief
> In low distress are laid,
> Soft be our hearts their pains to feel
> And swift our hands to aid.

Even more impressive, perhaps, is a hymn that occurs in three books: 'Jesus, my Lord, how rich Thy grace'. In the opening verses Doddridge laments that there is no way in which he can pay to Christ the debt he owes him.

> But Thou hast brethren here below
> The partners of Thy grace,
> And wilt confess their humble names
> Before Thy Father's face.
>
> In them Thou may'st be clothed and fed
> And visited and cheered;
> And in their accents of distress
> My Saviour's voice is heard.
>
> Thy face with reverence and with love
> I in Thy poor would see.
> O let me rather beg my bread
> Than hold it back from Thee!

Obvious also is the missionary note struck from time to time in his hymns, reflecting, be it always remembered, the content of his preaching. For example, in a hymn for 'A Day of Prayer for the Revival of Religion' his prayers cover the world:

> Loud let the Gospel trumpet blow
> And call the nations from afar;
> Let all the isles their Saviour know
> And be Thy love the leading star.

And in the next hymn in Humphrey's edition, on Isaiah 66.8, he stresses the same thought:

> Behold with pleasing ecstasy
> The Gospel standard lifted high,
> That all the nations far and near
> May in the great salvation share.

A most curious happening, not fully explained, made two of his hymns very familiar in Anglican circles. Five hymns were added to a 1791 edition of Tate and Brady's Psalms, then much used in the Church of England. It is said they were inserted by a university printer, a Mr J. Archdeacon, to fill up some blank pages. Being a dissenter he was not sufficiently careful in his selection. He chose 'High let us swell our tuneful notes' and 'My God and is Thy Table spread' by the nonconformist Doddridge, along with 'Hark the herald angels sing' by Charles Wesley, who was after all a good Anglican, though with some unfortunate habits, 'Awake my soul and with the sun' by Bishop Ken, and 'Christ from the dead is raised', a paraphrase of 1 Corinthians 15.20 by Tate and Brady. However the authorities raised no objection and the hymns continued to appear in later editions. 'My God and is Thy Table spread' appears to this day in the *English Hymnal* and *Hymns Ancient and Modern*, and the latter also retains 'High let us swell our tuneful notes', though it is in no other book.

One of his best hymns, in my judgment, has surprisingly found a place in only three books, a New Year hymn, 'Great God, we sing that mighty hand. By which supported still we stand.' Some little debate has arisen over the last two lines. Orton's version runs

>Our helper, God, in whom we trust
>In better worlds our souls shall boast.

Dr Routley[1] exclaims against the pedantry of those who spoil this for the sake of rhyme, and read, as in the *Church Hymnary*

>Our helper God, in whom we trust
>Shall keep our souls and guard our dust.

As he protests, this substitutes the grave for heaven as the Christian's goal. But Orton's version is not really good and according to Humphreys, and I believe him, what Doddridge really wrote was

>Our Helper-God, in whom we trust
>To better worlds shall raise our dust.

This is surely better than either of the others.

Another New Year hymn, of great beauty and skilful craftsmanship, has somehow escaped the notice of any of our recent editors. It is worth quoting in full, since it is not generally accessible.

---

[1]Nuttall, op. cit., p. 62.

> My Helper God! I bless His name;
> The same His power, His grace the same;
> The tokens of His friendly care
> Open and crown and close the Year.
>
> I midst a thousand dangers stand,
> Supported by His guardian hand,
> And see, when I survey my ways,
> Ten thousand monuments of praise.
>
> Thus far His arm hath led me on;
> Thus far I make His mercy known;
> And while I tread this desert land
> New mercies still new songs demand.
>
> My grateful soul, on Jordan's shore,
> Shall raise one sacred pillar more!
> Then bear to His bright courts above
> Memorials of immortal love.

It is noticeable in how many of the hymns Doddridge in the last verse 'lands us all in heaven', to quote Charles Wesley. Heaven certainly played, for both good and ill, a much greater part in the religion of our forefathers than it does with us today.

The most widely used of his hymns in modern books is 'Ye servants of the Lord', which is in seven of them. 'The active Christian', it is headed in Humphreys. Second in use, to be found in six, is 'O God of Bethel'. This is one of the three Doddridge hymns used by the Church of Scotland committee in preparing the 1781 edition of the *Paraphrases*, which follow the metrical Psalms at the end of the Scottish Bible. The other two are 'Hark the glad sound' and 'Father of peace'. It is the much altered and greatly improved Scottish version with which we are familiar today. The story is somewhat complicated. The hymn in manuscript was in the possession during Doddridge's life-time of Lady Frances Erskine, who became the wife of Colonel Gardiner, both intimate friends of the writer. From this copy it was included in the 1745 edition of the *Paraphrases*, much as it was in the 1737 original. It was largely rewritten by the Reverend John Logan, and with still further changes was included in the 1781 *Paraphrases*, of which committee Logan was a member. So its heredity is Doddridge, 1745 *Paraphrases*, Logan, 1781 *Paraphrases*. It is interesting to compare the original as given by Humphreys with the hymn as we now use it.

## Hark The Glad Sound!

O God of Jacob, by whose hand
    Thine Israel still is fed,
Who through this weary pilgrimage
    Hath all our fathers led;
To Thee our humble vows we raise,
    To Thee address our prayer,
And in Thy kind and faithful breast
    Deposit all our care.
If Thou, through each perplexing path,
    Wilt be our constant Guide;
If Thou wilt daily bread supply
    And raiment wilt provide;
If Thou wilt spread Thy shield around
    Till these our wanderings cease,
And at our Father's loved abode
    Our souls arrive in peace;
To Thee, as to our Covenant God
    We will ourselves resign
And count that not our tenth alone
    But all we have is Thine.

'Hark the glad sound! The Saviour comes', a vigorous and triumphant Advent hymn, is also in the Scottish *Paraphrases* and in six modern hymnals. It is one of the great English hymns and perhaps the most widely used of any he wrote. One verse is admittedly based on lines in Pope's *Messiah*:

He from thick films shall purge the visual ray
And on the sightless eyeballs pour the day.

It is said that the Prince Consort chose 'O happy day that fixed my choice' for use at confirmation services in his family, but it has disappeared from present-day Anglican hymnals, though still popular elsewhere.

'Father of peace' was also improved for the *Paraphrases* and appears in that form in four modern books. It is much used and greatly loved in Scotland.

Passing over several other hymns which appear in one or two current hymnals but are not generally known, I feel that 'God of my life, through all my days' deserves a place in more than the *Methodist Hymn Book,* for both its poetry and its substance, though perhaps it is not suitable for singing in an average congregation. It is said to have been written in his last days in 1751.

I quote the closing verses:

> When death o'er nature shall prevail
>   And all the powers of language fail,
> Joy through my swimming eyes shall break
>   And mean the thanks I cannot speak.
>
> But O when that last conflict's o'er,
>   And I am chained to flesh no more,
> With what glad accents shall I rise
>   To join the music of the skies.
>
> Soon shall I learn the exalted strains,
>   Which echo through the heavenly plains:
> And emulate with joy unknown
>   The glowing seraphs round Thy throne.
>
> The cheerful tribute will I give
>   Long as a deathless soul can live;
> A work so sweet, a theme so high
>   Demands and crowns eternity.

And on what more appropriate note could we leave Philip Doddridge?

# 3

## BORN IN SONG

### *John (1703-91) and Charles (1707-88) Wesley and the Hymns of Methodism*

MANY volumes have been written on the work of the Wesleys and many more on their hymns; as they richly deserve. Charles Wesley is certainly the second name, and some would say the first, in English hymnody. No one has so many hymns in common use today, and if quantity as well as quality is considered, he has no rival. And apart from their religious and literary merit his hymns are notable as the battle songs of a spiritual revolution. So vast is the literature about the Wesleys that any man might well feel there was nothing more to be said; at any rate nothing more that *he* could say. But it would be unthinkable to omit them from such a volume as this. I cannot claim that I have any new contribution to make, and Methodist and other expert readers, if I have any, must forgive my recitation of some part of an oft-repeated story for the benefit of the less enlightened. Those who are not familiar with John Wesley's *Journal* are urged to read it, or parts of it, without delay.[1]

I make no attempt to paint once more the dark background of the condition of England in the beginning of the eighteenth century, or to assess the part played by Methodism, not only in leading thousands to a living faith and in reviving the life of the Churches, but also in bringing light and healing to the national life as a whole, stimulating social reform and raising moral standards. Nor need I do more than remind the reader of the heroic labours of the two brothers themselves, stemming from the overpowering religious awakening that came to them both in 1738. It is difficult to be sure what was wrong with them before that. They came from a remarkable family and had a Christian

---

[1] I may be allowed to refer to my own edition of *Selections* in the Treasury of Christian Books, SCM Press, as a convenient one.

home and training. At Oxford they showed zeal beyond their fellows. Their devotion took them to work in a strange land only to be reached after a perilous voyage. Yet they were both failures in America. Both returned to England defeated and disillusioned with themselves, Charles first, but soon followed by John. John had shown a singular lack of wisdom in more directions than one: his rigid churchmanship and intolerant concern for rites and ceremonies had won him many enemies. Theirs was a painstaking, dutiful and methodical religion. They had tried very hard. They had disciplined themselves and others. They had kept themselves unspotted from the world. Yet somehow there was no life in it: 'Faultily faultless, icily regular, splendidly null.'[1]

But the day came when John felt his heart 'strangely warmed' as he listened to 'one reading Luther's Preface to the Epistle to the Romans' at a meeting, 'very unwillingly' attended in Aldersgate Street. And then all things became new, as they had for brother Charles only a few days before. They 'passed out of the state of the anxious and conscientious servant into the glorious liberty of the child of God.'[2] The result for John, or part of it, was that 'for more than half a century he laboured, through evil report and good report, to speed what he believed to be the everlasting Gospel, travelling more miles, preaching more sermons, publishing more books of a practical sort, and making more converts, than any man of his day, or perhaps of any day, and dying at last, March 2, 1791, in harness, at the patriarchal age of 88.'[3]

Here we are concerned with only one aspect of the lives of these many-sided geniuses—hymnody. One of the chief expressions and instruments of the Methodist revival was hymn singing. 'Methodism was born in song,' says the preface to the 1933 *Methodist Hymn Book*. Both John, and apparently Charles also,[4] wrote hymns in Georgia before their great awakening, but from the moment that this unlocked the springs hymns poured out from Charles in an unbroken stream right to the end of his long life. It is interesting to note in passing that Charles was born in 1707, the year when Watts published his epoch-making *Hymns*

---

[1] Tennyson, *Maud*.
[2] *The Hymn Book of the Modern Church*, A. E. Gregory, p. 158.
[3] J. H. Overton, Julian's *Dictionary of Hymnology*, p. 1257.
[4] The wife of Governor Oglethorpe in Georgia, wrote: 'Mr Wesley has the gift of verse and has written many sweet hymns, which we sing'. J. Telford, *Charles Wesley*, p. 245.

*and Spiritual Songs.* John had been born four and a half years earlier.

The beginnings of John's new spiritual life and the beginnings of his concern with hymnody were both due to his contact with Moravians. On the voyage out to Georgia he had the company of a group of Moravian emigrants. They impressed him by their calmness in a storm, their cheerful faith, their helpful spirit—and their hymn singing. On the third day of the voyage he began to learn German in order to be able to talk with them and soon took part in their daily worship. It was a new kind of hymn singing to him and he began to study their hymn book, the *Gesang-Buch*, published the previous year, 1735, by Zinzendorf for their community at Herrnhut. Wesley translated some of them. Perhaps already on the voyage he started to compile the hymn book he published in Georgia. One of the many charges brought against him by the Grand Jury for Savannah in August, 1737, was his use in church of unauthorized hymns.

He was only thirty-four when he published that Charlestown hymnal for the use of his congregation there, a crudely printed volume of seventy-four pages containing seventy hymns. Half came from Isaac Watts, six from George Herbert, two from Addison, fifteen from the Wesley family, five of them from Samuel senior, his father, five from Samuel junior, his elder brother, and five from the German by John himself. There were none from Charles, who was by this time back in England after only six months in Georgia. This was the first of Wesley's long series of hymn books, and the first published by anybody in America.

'The poetical publications of John and Charley Wesley, jointly or separately', says Benson,[1] 'cover a period of fifty-three years and number fifty-six (excluding tune books); the contents of not less than thirty-six of these are exclusively original, with much original work appearing in the collective volumes.' It is an amazing record. Outstanding among them all is the 1780 volume, *A Collection of Hymns for the use of the People called Methodists,* with a notable preface, containing a selection of the best of the hymns of Charles, a number by John, and several from other sources, including Watts.

It is sometimes said that John was the administrator, leader,

---

[1] p. 230.

and evangelist of the movement, while Charles was the hymn writer. There is a measure of truth in this, but it is much too sweeping a statement. Both of the brothers gave themselves to 'field preaching' and Charles was as doughty an evangelist as John, though he did not continue his travelling so long. Both wrote hymns. John was a hymnwriter of great distinction and the editor of the 1780 book. Whether deliberately or not the brothers did not make clear the authorship of their hymns: many are in books bearing the names of both with no distinguishing mark, and it is impossible to allocate them with any certainty, though it is not disputed that Charles wrote by far the larger number. Dr Bett in *The Hymns of Methodism,* a work of great value to all students, reckons that there are thirty-four translations by John, from German, French and Spanish, and also names sixteen original hymns which in his judgment, based on internal evidence, are probably by John, though he has not convinced all the other experts.

John was a brilliant translator, and a skilful editor. For the 1780 volume he chose the best from the great mass of Charles' work, eliminating the weak verses and not hesitating to use his blue pencil. Charles wrote much poor stuff, unworthy of his genius, and does not seem to have had much power of self-criticism. John tempered his tendency to emotional excess and sensuous imagery, which he had perhaps learned from the Moravians. For all his debt to the Moravians John felt compelled to break with them later, partly owing to their quietism, which made some go the length of giving up Bible reading, the sacraments and prayer, because salvation did not lie in them and they might come to rely too much on these *means* of grace, and partly because of the unhappy eccentricities of Zinzendorf and others in applying terms of endearment to our Lord and dwelling in morbid detail on the physical sufferings on the Cross. To anything of the kind John was acutely sensitive. In his own work he shows a dignity and restraint which is sometimes lacking in Charles, whose hymns probably owe much to his brother's criticism. John was indeed never reluctant to exercise his revising zeal on other people's work, sometimes with very unhappy results, as at times with Herbert and Watts, though he very much resented any interference with his own.

Among his translations are some of our greatest treasures. In his valuable book on the German hymn writers, Sydney Moore says of 'Commit thou all thy griefs', Wesley's version of Paul Gerhardt's *Befiehl du deine wege* that 'merely to read it through line by line alongside the original is a revelation as to the high art of translation.'[1] Emerson and Oliver Wendell Holmes agreed in regarding 'Thou hidden love of God', from Tersteegen, as 'the supreme hymn'. All the churches have recognized the merits of 'Jesus, Thy boundless love', 'Lo God is here', and 'Now I have found the ground'. In hymnody, as in many other realms, we owe John Wesley more than we realize.

The 1780 *Collection* is among the greatest books of Christendom. But extravagant praise does no service to the Christian cause or to the memory of Charles, who is great enough not to need it. John Wesley himself began the bad habit in his preface. After making it clear that only a small part is by himself, he claims: '1. In these hymns there is no doggerel, no botches; nothing put in to patch up the rhyme; no feeble expletives. 2. Here is nothing turgid or bombast, on the one hand, or low and creeping on the other. 3. Here are no cant expressions, no words without meaning. Those who impute this to us know not what they say. We talk common sense, both in prose and verse, and use no word but in a fixed and determinate sense. 4. Here are, allow me to say, both the purity, the strength, and the elegance of the English language; and at the same time, the utmost simplicity and plainness, suited to every capacity. Lastly, I desire men of taste to judge (these are the only competent judges) whether there be not in some of the following hymns the true spirit of poetry, such as cannot be acquired by art and labour, but must be the gift of nature.' A little later he begs that any who wish to reprint the hymns will 'print them just as they are. But I desire they would not attempt to mend them—for they really are not able. None of them is able to mend either the sense or the verse'. Here, in short, is perfection.

Bernard Manning goes even further, if that were possible. In *The Hymns of Wesley and Watts,* a book sparkling with wit and abounding in passages of deep insight, he asserts, speaking of the 1780 *Collection* (p. 14): 'You may think my language about the hymns extravagant: therefore I repeat it in stronger terms. This little book ranks in Christian literature with the Psalms, the Book

[1]*Sursum Corda*, p. 75.

of Common Prayer, the Canon of the Mass. In one way it is perfect, unapproachable, elemental in its perfection. You cannot alter it except to mar it; it is a work of supreme devotional art by a religious genius.' With all respect to the memory of a friend of great ability and understanding, and in spite of his saying it twice, I still think this is grossly extravagant. And indeed in later pages Manning makes clear that he does not really believe the *Collection* to be beyond criticism or improvement. Language so sweeping as this drives one to say that it would be possible to fill pages of this book with faulty rhymes, awkward constructions and extravagant expressions, to say nothing of the more debatable ground of the theological balance of the book, and of Charles Wesley's hymns in particular. But that it is 'a work of supreme devotional art by a religious genius', I cordially agree.

Without making any exhaustive search one finds him rhyming guest and feast, array'd and head, receive and live, glass and race, compel and feel, give and grief. And one wonders how the editor passed this, in Hymn 20:

> Turn to Jesus crucified.
> Fly to those dear wounds of His,
> Sink into the purple flood.

After a number of hymns in his ecstatic, exclamatory style it is with relief that one comes upon the more sober, objective note of Isaac Watts, in, for example, 'O God, our help', though one is annoyed by the unhappy editorial change from 'Our God'.[1] It is indeed no cause for surprise, or even for criticism unless provoked by adulation, that so prolific a writer should sometimes blunder or have his off days. There are poor pages in the works of all the great poets. Charles is credited with having written as many as 6,500 hymns, though a considerable proportion of them are brief scriptural annotations. Yet no writer is known to have written more, and—this is the real cause for wonder—no writer has a larger number of hymns in common use even today, after 170 years. It is, perhaps, not surprising that the present edition of the *Methodist Hymn Book*, even after the drastic pruning of the earlier editions, should still contain 243 of Charles Wesley's hymns.[2] No one else is in sight; Isaac Watts is nearest, limping in with a mere forty-three. But *Congregational Praise*, with no family ties to consider, contains forty-five by Charles Wesley,

---

[1] It is oddly classified under 'Describing Death'.
[2] The 1904 edition had 429.

running Watts closely with his forty-eight. The nearest after that is Montgomery with twenty-two. The new *Baptist Hymn Book* includes thirty-six from Wesley and twenty-six from Watts with no one else in reach. In *Hymns Ancient and Modern,* 1950, J. M. Neale tops the list with fifty-six, but Wesley has thirty-two. The Presbyterian *Church Hymnary* reverses the order, giving Wesley twenty-four and Neale twenty-three, but these two easily lead all others. Even the *English Hymnal* includes twenty, and *Songs of Praise* twenty-one. These figures are a remarkable tribute to Charles Wesley.

John Wesley claimed that the *Collection* was 'a little body of experimental and practical divinity'. 'The hymns are carefully ranged under proper heads, according to the experience of real Christians.' The table of Contents is indeed unique. 'Part I. Exhorting sinners to return to God. Describing the pleasantness of religion; the goodness of God; Death; Judgment; Heaven; Hell; Praying for a Blessing. Part II. Describing formal and inward religion. Part III. Praying for Repentance; for mourners convinced of sin; for persons convinced of backsliding; for backsliders recovered. Part IV. For Believers Rejoicing, Fighting, Praying, Watching, Working, Suffering; Seeking for full Redemption, Saved, Interceding for the World. Part V. For the Society Meeting. Giving thanks, Praying, Parting.' Compare that with the Contents of a modern hymnal. Take, for example, the current *Methodist Hymn Book*. 'Adoration and Worship; God, the Holy Trinity; in Creation and Providence; His Love in Redemption; The Lord Jesus Christ. His glory, name and praise, His incarnation, His life, teaching and example; His suffering and ascension; His priesthood and sympathy; His Kingdom, present and future: The Holy Spirit: The Holy Scriptures: The Gospel Call: The Christian Life; Repentance and Forgiveness, Faith and Regeneration, Dedication, Joy, and Thanksgiving, Love and Communion, Temptation and Conflict, Trustfulness and Peace, Prayer, Christian Holiness, Service and Influence, Pilgrimage, Guidance, Perseverance, Death, Judgment, The Future Life: The Church, The Lord's Day; Worship in the Sanctuary; Privileges and Security of Christ's Church; The Communion of Saints; The Sacraments; Marriage; Ministers and Teachers; Missions at home and abroad; The Church Militant and Triumphant: For Little Children: School and Work: Home and Family Worship: National and Social Life: Times and Seasons.'

The difference is striking and significant. It is not unfair to say that in the *Collection* attention is concentrated almost exclusively upon the individual soul. 'In what other publication of the kind', enquires the Preface, 'have you so distinct and full an account of scriptural Christianity: such a declaration of the heights and depths of religion, speculative and practical: so strong cautions against the most plausible errors, particularly those that are most prevalent? and so clear directions for making your calling and election sure; for perfecting holiness in the fear of God?' Would it be going too far to choose as its motto the lines from Charles Wesley's Hymn 44:

> Nothing is worth a thought beneath
> But how I may escape the death
>    That never, never dies!
> How make my own election sure,
> And when I fail on earth, secure
>    A mansion in the skies.

The modern book lays its emphasis on God in Christ and His great deeds for our redemption. It has much to say about the Church and about Christian discipleship in national and social life. It is not only a question of contrasting then and now: the approach of Isaac Watts is also quite different. His hymns characteristically arise from meditation on the majesty of God Himself in creation, providence and redemption. Their emphasis is objective while Wesley's by comparison is subjective. In Wesley there is a more spontaneous fervour. His hymns come rushing out of him; they are the fruit of personal experience. He just can't help singing. 'Experience' and 'feeling' are often the words, and nearly always the thoughts, on his lips.

Wesley has not got Watts' sense—at any rate he does not give it expression—of the cosmic significance of Christ's redemption. He has no eyes for God's world of nature and its changing seasons, and has next to nothing to say about the influence of Christian discipleship in the life of society. *The Methodist Hymn Book* devotes much space to such themes, in harmony with the leading part which that Church has always taken in this field, but one cannot help noticing that Charles Wesley, who is omnipresent in the rest of the volume, is here represented by only one hymn on 'world peace and brotherhood', and even that looks as if it was a stray from another section! 'Wesley', declares Bernard Manning, 'is obsessed with one theme, God and the Soul; for the stage in space and time on which the drama is set he has little concern. He is always at Calvary; no other place in the universe matters, and for him the course of historic time is lost in the eternal Now'.[1] He would have had no patience with what Manning calls the 'vaguely religious poetizing' which fills so much of our hymn books.

I am not of course being so silly as to suggest that Wesley's concentration on the psychology of the soul meant that his faith was anything but Christo-centric, or that he did not believe as wholeheartedly as Watts in the fundamental verities of Christian doctrine. There is indeed in Wesley a didactic, dogmatic proclamation of doctrine, of the Holy Trinity, the Incarnation, and our Redemption by the Cross. He is as far as possible from being a pedlar of humanistic amiabilities.

> Let earth and heaven combine,
> Angels and men agree,
> To praise in songs divine
> The incarnate Deity,
> Our God contracted to a span,
> Incomprehensibly made man.

It is notable that he has supplied us with some of the most widely familiar hymns on the great events of the Christian Year: 'Hark, the herald angels sing' for Christmas; 'Christ the Lord is risen today' for Easter; 'Hail the day that sees Him rise' for the Ascension; 'Come Thou everlasting Spirit' and 'Away with our fears' for Whitsun; and for Good Friday, 'And can it be that I should gain', 'All ye that pass by', and 'O Thou who hast redeemed of old'. With Charles Wesley's help, 'Methodism has always been able to sing its creed.'[2] But for all that one cannot miss the difference of approach, and in it lies both the strength and the weakness of Charles Wesley.

The lack of provision for the Sacraments and other functions of a Church in the *Collection*, which was supplied in the 'Additional Hymns' after Wesley's death, was due to the fact that he did not think of his 'societies' as churches, but as meetings for evangelism and the deepening of the spiritual life. The provision for infant baptism, the ministry and other matters of church order is still more apparent in the 'Supplement' of 1830. The logic of facts is being recognized.

---

[1] Op. cit., p. 43.   [2] Preface to the 1933 *Methodist Hymn Book*.

Much of the *Collection* is an introspective analysis of the stages of Christian experience. Every mood of the Christian soul is reflected. Benson's comment is a just description of many of the hymns. 'Instead of a congregation uttering its corporate praise with a common voice, we have a gathering of individuals conducting their private devotions in audible unison.'[1] His hymns are 'I' hymns and not 'we' hymns, as the Germans put it: *ich* not *wir*. Many have been judged by most compilers of hymnals to be too intense, emotional and intimate for general use and have not been used outside Methodism. It was only after John's death that 'Jesus, lover of my soul' was admitted even to the Methodist book. After commenting on this exclusion Ellerton says: 'All who have really felt its wonderful power and reality would wish to see it in a church hymnal, yet most clergymen, I suppose, would hesitate before selecting it as the vehicle of the ordinary worship of a mixed congregation.'[2] There is throughout his writings the intimacy of intense personal feeling, a record of personal experience, of what has happened to himself. It inevitably follows that many of the hymns are not really intelligible to those who have not gone through such an experience, and to put them on the lips of a miscellaneous congregation is to encourage insincerity.

Watts was fully capable of intense devotional fervour and depth, but he deliberately tried in his hymns to keep to a common level of education and experience and refused to spread his wings and soar out of sight of the congregation. He stresses personal religion, self-dedication, dependence, but there is a different note in Wesley, what Ellerton calls 'the yet deeper cries of the dark and cheerless heart for the light and warmth of communion with its Lord'.[3] We have need of both Wesley and Watts. They supplement one another.

Wesley's hymns, as the Preface says, are 'an account of scriptural Christianity'. The 'Table of Texts' in the *Collection* reveals how few parts of the Bible are neglected, and some chapters are commented upon almost verse by verse. The total of his hymns is considerably increased, as mentioned earlier, by the 2,030 verses in his *Short Hymns on Select Passages of the Holy Scriptures*. A careful examination of any of his best known hymns will reveal numerous Scripture references. Luke Wiseman[4] has found

[1] Op. cit., p. 250.
[2] *John Ellerton*, Henry Housman, SPCK, 1896, p. 236f. [3] Housman, p. 203.
[4] *Charles Wesley*, Epworth Press, p. 211.

twenty-three in the sixteen lines of 'O Thou who camest from above'. Dr Bett has pointed out that in the four lines

> Thou of life the fountain art,
>    Freely let me take of Thee;
> Spring Thou up within my heart,
>    Rise to all eternity.

there are clear references to Psalm 26.9, Rev. 22.17, Numbers 21.17, John 4.14. Charles Wesley's thought and language were steeped in the Bible, and not only in the Authorized Version: some of the references do not become clear until we realize that he is thinking of the original Greek. Scripture is woven into the very fabric; it is no adding of text to text. It is the thought of the Bible and not only its phrases that find expression.

Wesley's hymns are also evangelistic weapons and reflect the work of an evangelist. He evangelized wherever he could find an opportunity: in the churches until the pulpits were closed to him; in the prisons; in the 'fields'. One extraordinary story tells of his winning ten prisoners in Newgate in July, 1738, all under sentence of death. He spent a night with them in the cells, administered Communion, went with them in the cart to the place of execution. 'It was one of the most triumphant hours I have ever known', he wrote in his *Journal*. His evangelical preaching offended the people at the Islington church where he was curate, and he had to leave the only Anglican appointment he ever held, though he remained loyal to the Church of England all his life. He took to the open air, like Whitefield and brother John, and preached to enormous crowds in Moorfield or Kennington Common, and his travels led him during twenty years throughout the land. In many places he was stoned and assaulted, and on several occasions the meeting houses in which he preached were sacked by the mob. It is against such a background that many of his hymns were written and must be read. They both grew out of and served the evangelism. Hymn after hymn has its urgent, direct appeal. In the first hymn he wrote after his spiritual awakening, 'Where shall my wandering soul begin?', after rendering thanks for his own deliverance, he asserts his purpose to carry the good news to others:

> Outcasts of men, to you I call,
>    Harlots and publicans and thieves!
> He spreads His arms to embrace you all;
>    Sinners alone His grace receive.

     .    .    .    .    .

Come, O my guilty brethren come!

Here lies another of the striking differences between his hymns and those of Watts. Both, I suspect, by temperament and certainly through ill-health Watts was incapable of such evangelistic work. Where the Wesleys reached out to the common people, the unchurched masses, Watts led a quiet, sheltered life in a wealthy and artistic circle, and set himself in his *Psalms and Hymns* to meet the needs of the settled, worshipping congregation. It was a task that greatly needed doing and in saying this I am not hinting at any criticism of Watts. His disabling ill-health was far from imaginary.

Wesley's message was the availability of salvation for everybody. Sometimes in the *Collection* the words 'for all' are printed in italics or capitals. There is a reflection here of the relentless war the Wesleys waged against the doctrines of extreme Calvinism, which taught 'double predestination', that is, that some were chosen by God for salvation, while others were left to damnation, outside the exercise of His mercy.[1] The great strength of Calvinism lay in its assertion of the sovereign majesty of God and of the utter dependence of the creature upon the Creator, of the sinner upon the wholly unmerited, pardoning grace of God. It was right in asserting that salvation could come to anybody only through the mercy of God and never through human merit. It was dreadfully wrong in declaring that any man was outside the reach of His love, as some Calvinists did declare. Considerable sections of the churches were already Arminian, as those were called who believed in the availability of salvation to all, after the theologian Arminius. But the influence of the Wesleys made a powerful contribution to the debate, and the old controversy, then fierce and divisive, is now a thing of the past. Nowhere does Charles Wesley nail his colours to the mast more firmly than in this hymn:

> Father, whose everlasting love,
>   Thy only Son for sinners gave,
> Whose grace to all did freely move
>   And sent Him down the world to save.
> Help us Thy mercy to extol,
>   Immense, unfathomed, unconfined;
> To praise the Lamb who died for all,
> The general Saviour of mankind.

---

[1] See pp. 23, 75f.

> Thy undistinguishing regard
> Was cast on Adam's fallen race;
> For all Thou hast in Christ prepared
> Sufficient, sovereign, saving grace.
>
> The world He suffered to redeem;
> For all He hath atonement made;
> For those who will not come to Him
> The ransom of His life was paid.
>
> Arise, O God, maintain Thy cause!
> The fullness of the Gentiles call;
> Lift up the standard of Thy Cross
> And all shall own Thou diedst for all.

Hardly a line of this hymn is without its assertion of the universality of God's offer of redemption, unequivocally proclaimed in this verse of another (*MHB* 49) in praise of God's 'ceaseless, unexhausted love':

> It streams the whole creation through,
> So plenteous is the store;
> Enough for all, enough for each,
> Enough for evermore.

Many more might be quoted to the same effect.

Not so obvious to the casual reader is the emphasis in the *Collection* on 'Christian Perfection' as attainable in this life, a doctrine vigorously disputed by other schools of belief. As an aspiration no Christian could aim at less: 'Be ye perfect, as your heavenly Father is perfect.' It was the possibility of its practical attainment in this life by sinful men, 'at once sinful and saved' as the Calvinist put it, which was in question. Looking back, it seems as if the dispute, in part at least, was a matter of defining terms. By sin, in this connection, John Wesley meant 'a voluntary violation of a known law of God', while his opponents were thinking of the deep-seated disease of the human heart and not only of deliberate acts of disobedience. 'By perfection,' said John Wesley, 'I mean the humble patient love of God and our neighbour ruling our words and actions.' His critics were right to deny that men, at least on earth, could ever be holy in the sight of God. The Wesleys were equally right in urging that we must not be content with 'Justification' but must press on, with God's help, in 'Sanctification'; which no properly instructed Calvinist would have challenged for a moment! But some statements, on both sides, were certainly open to misunderstanding. Here is Charles Wesley in combative mood:

> Let others hug their chains;
> For sin and Satan plead,
> And say, from sin's remains
> They never can be freed.
> Rejoice in hope, rejoice with me!
> We shall from all our sins be free.

He prays for

> The joys of holiness below
> And then the joys of heaven.

Or again,
> What is our calling, glorious hope,
> But inward holiness?
> When Jesus makes my heart His home
> My sin shall all depart;
> And lo, He saith, I quickly come,
> To fill and rule thy heart!
> Be it according to Thy word!
> Redeem me from all sin;
> My heart would now receive Thee, Lord;
> Come in, my Lord, come in!

Wesley has hymns sounding a practical determined note, like 'Soldiers of Christ, arise', but there are also hymns of a more mystical mood in which he grapples with profundities, as in 'let earth and heaven combine', quoted above. It is, I think, a misuse of words to call either of the brothers 'mystics' in any technical sense. Indeed, John broke with his one-time hero, William Law, when he turned mystic and took to what Wesley described as the 'sublime nonsense' of Boehme's teachings. But there is at times what we may call, for want of a better word, a mystical quality in the hymns. It is to be seen in the famous 'wrestling Jacob', which is a remarkable poem, though in spite of the judgment of many better men I cannot regard it as a good *hymn,* or as at all suitable for congregational use:

> Come, O Thou Traveller unknown,
> Whom still I hold, but cannot see.

It sounds in the hymn 'Come, Holy Ghost, all quickening fire.'

> Eager for Thee I ask and pant,
> So strong the principle divine,
> Carries me out with sweet constraint
> Till all my hallowed soul is Thine;

> Plunged in the Godhead's deepest sea
> And lost in Thine immensity.

So he prays in 'Master, I own Thy lawful claim',

> Flow back the rivers to the sea
> And let our all be lost in Thee!

He is perpetually amazed at the divine paradoxes of the Incarnation (*MHB* 134)

> Emptied of His majesty
> Of His dazzling glories shorn,
> Being's source begins to be,
> And God Himself is born!

He hails with wonder (*MHB* 325)

> Th' o'erwhelming power of saving grace,
> The sight that veils the seraph's face,
> The speechless awe that does not move,
> And all the silent heaven of love.

And there is that very deep hymn (*MHB* 371)

> And can it be that I should gain
> An interest in the Saviour's blood?

As we have seen, Watts maintained that the ornaments of poetry must be excluded from hymns. John Wesley, on the other hand, believed that a good hymn should be a lyric poem, and, with justification, made high claims for the poetic quality of those in the *Collection*, though elsewhere he said of his brother's hymns that 'some are good, some mean, some most excellently good'. Without going so far as to assert that Charles Wesley never nodded, the sheer virtuosity of his poetic skill and handling of the English language must not be left unnoticed. For good reasons, Watts confined himself for the most part to the three most familiar psalm metres: Wesley is said to have used thirty. Students of his writings have noted his expert use of all the literary devices of alliteration, assonance, chiasmus, metaphor and the like. There is a craftsmanship in his hymns, though it is not obtrusive and in general his speech is direct and penetrating and does not deal in abstractions. To read a large number of his hymns in succession is to be impressed by the amazing variety of theme and of literary presentation. Both brothers were men of wide learning and culture, and drew upon the secular literature of the past as well as on the Bible, as Dr Bett has demonstrated at length in *The Hymns of Methodism*. Occasionally the classical references are too erudite for ordinary readers and sometimes the words are unduly polysyllabic, but not often.

As Dr Johnson would say, writers are not on their oath when they pen obituary notices or 'lapidary inscriptions', yet the evidence confirms the words on Charles Wesley's memorial tablet in the City Road Chapel which declare that he was 'learned without pride, and pious without ostentation'. And Luke Wiseman[1] quotes from the preface which his wife wrote for a posthumous volume of his sermons: 'His most striking excellence was humility; it extended to his talents as well as his virtues; he not only acknowledged and pointed out but delighted in the superiority of another, and if ever there was a human being who disliked power, avoided pre-eminence, and shrank from praise, it was Charles Wesley.'

But what he shrank from we cannot forbear to render. In Charles Wesley, as Dr George Sampson has expressed it, there arrived 'a new religious poet of burning sincerity, of high poetic feeling, of daring force of expression, and of intensely characteristic style'[2] and what he would have valued most, of still undiminished power to quicken and maintain the spiritual life of millions.

[1] p. 230.
[2] *The Century of Divine Song*, p. 15.

# 4

# GOD'S MYSTERIOUS WAY

*The strange stories of William Cowper (1731-1800)
and John Newton (1725-1807)*

THE life of Cowper[1] is a heart-rending tragedy. That gentle, kind, deeply religious personality was overshadowed by almost life-long gloom. Periods of placid happiness and creative activity were broken into by recurrent attacks of melancholic madness. The man who wrote some of the loveliest hymns ever penned, which have brought comfort and encouragement to untold millions, came to believe that God had cast him off, and died in 'unutterable despair', rejecting all words of consolation and hope. A thin-skinned creature at best, he was the recipient of blow after blow of misfortune and bereavement that would have tested the faith and stamina of the strongest.

Born in 1731 in his father's rectory in Berkhamstead in Hertfordshire, then a village of about 1,500 inhabitants, he came of a family of some distinction. His father was the son of a judge and the nephew of a Lord Chancellor. On his mother's side he was descended from the poet Donne, one time Dean of St Paul's, a fact in which Cowper took great pride. When he was only six his mother died in giving birth to his brother John. As through his tears he watched the funeral moving off, his nurse foolishly assured him that his mother would come back tomorrow. But she never did.

Little knowing what he was doing, his father decided to send the delicate, timid child to a boarding school. To be torn so young from mother and home would be a stern enough ordeal for any child, let alone for one so sensitive. In his poem *Tirocinium*[2]

---

[1] It appears to be established that the name was originally spelled Cooper and was so pronounced by the family.

[2] i.e., apprenticeship.

Cowper protests against the cruelty of so sending children away from home with a parting that 'lacerates' the heart. To add to his misery he was mercilessly bullied by an older lout. 'I had such a dread of him that I did not dare lift my eyes to his face. I knew him best by his shoe buckle.' After two years of this torture the bully was expelled and Cowper was removed from the school. Surely here already, before he was eight years old, were experiences enough to break his nerve and to convince him that life was unfriendly. Some eye trouble led to his spending the next two years with an oculist, where he was not allowed to read, and no doubt had too much time to brood. A happier stage came in 1741 when he went to Westminster School. Here he apparently did well both in the classroom and at games. He made friends and seemed to be re-establishing himself.

On leaving there at the age of eighteen he was sent by his father to learn law in a solicitor's office in Holborn, where he lived in, a fellow pupil being Edward Thurlow, a future Lord Chancellor and a very different type of man. Cowper had no liking for the law, but the legal tradition was in the family and no doubt this was thought to be the most promising career for him. Intensely bored, he wasted his time for three years in trifling, nothing worse but nothing better. His one refuge was in a close friendship with his uncle's family in Southampton Row, where there were two lively and attractive girls, Harriet and Theodora, with the second of whom he fell in love. But after two years of courtship her father forbade an engagement, partly because he disapproved of the marriage of cousins, and partly because he had his doubts about William, and his ability to 'support a wife'.[1] They never met again, but Theodora did not marry and kept Cowper's letters to her until her death at the age of ninety. She used to send him gifts and contributed to his support anonymously, though it is hard to believe that Cowper did not guess the identity of 'dear anonymous', as he called the donor.

For nine years Cowper played at being a lawyer. He was called to the Bar and had chambers in the Middle and Inner Temple. He secured no briefs but held a minor position as a Commissioner

---

[1] It seems that Theodora herself was subject to fits of melancholy and mentally unstable. This may have been recognized by her father and have been another reason for forbidding the marriage. See *William Cowper of the Inner Temple, Esq.*, Charles Ryskamp, Cambridge University Press, 1959, p. 124.

## God's Mysterious Way

of Bankruptcy, which had few duties but brought in £60 a year, and went in for some desultory journalism. All his life Cowper was greatly dependent on human affection, yet in the same year as the breaking off of his engagement, his father died and he lost his closest friend by drowning. His slender capital was nearly exhausted and he was obviously a failure at his profession. It was a dismal outlook. Then luck apparently turned his way. Through the influence of a relation he was offered a clerkship in the House of Lords, which would have meant the end of financial troubles. But the offer drove him into a panic. Was he capable of doing the job? And he had to face an interview with a committee before the appointment could be confirmed. The prospect weighed upon his mind. In sober truth he nearly 'worried himself to death', for when the time for the interview came near he attempted suicide. He considered in turn laudanum, drowning in the Thames, and a penknife, though none of these attempts was very determined. But he did nearly succeed in hanging himself. All this led to a complete mental breakdown. There could be no question of his taking the clerkship and he had to resign even his commissionership.

In December, 1763, his friends sent him to a private asylum in St Albans kept by a Dr Cotton. Cotton was himself something of a poet, and five of his hymns appeared in various English and American hymn books.[1] A sensible, kindly, Christian man, and skilled in his profession according to the knowledge of his day, his methods of treatment were in happy contrast to many then in vogue. Under his care Cowper gradually quietened down and began to emerge from his gloom.

Up to this time Cowper's religion had apparently, and by his own confession, been merely conventional. Certainly his pursuits and associations had not been evangelical. But now he experienced a religious awakening. Here is his own account. 'Having risen with somewhat of a more cheerful feeling I repaired to my room where breakfast waited for me. While I sat at table I found the cloud of horror which had so long hung over me was every moment passing away. I flung myself into a chair near the window and seeing a Bible there ventured once more to apply to it for

---

[1] He was a friend of Doddridge. Doubtless on Cotton's suggestion Cowper read his *Rise and Progress of Religion in the Soul*, and later wrote, 'Next to the Word itself' Doddridge's books 'are my daily bread' (*Memoir*, p. 59f.).

comfort and instruction. The first verse I saw was the 25th of the III Romans, "Whom God hath set forth to be a propitiation through faith in his blood, to declare his righteousness for the remission of sins that are past, through the forbearance of God". Immediately I received strength to believe it, and the full beams of the Sun's righteousness shone upon me. I saw the sufficiency of the atonement He had made, my pardon sealed in His blood, and all the fulness and completeness of His justification. In a moment I believed and received the Gospel. . . . Unless the almighty arms had been under me I think I should have died of gratitude and joy.' The story recalls Augustine's similar experience of conversion in the garden at Milan.

Mr Faussett in his biography is not impressed. It was, he says, only an emotional experience in which the real William Cowper was not involved. 'His conversion was not really a rebirth into a new life and a new consciousness but only a transformation of his rigid fear into melting acquiescence. . . . His relation to God was, in fact, still servile and fatalistic'.[1] Mr Faussett, in fact, takes the line that Cowper was too intelligent a man to believe in such nonsense as Christianity, though he inconsistently maintains in the same breath that it was his belief in it that drove him mad! To this subject we shall return.

Whatever the explanation, the fact remains that Cowper was a changed man. His new-found faith absorbed him and he could think and speak of nothing else. For the first time he felt completely normal and at peace. He had escaped out of the net of the fowler, or as he himself wrote in a later day:

> I was a stricken deer that left the herd
> Long since; with many an arrow deep infixed
> My panting side was charged, when I withdrew
> To seek a tranquil death in distant shades.
> There was I found by One who had Himself
> Been hurt by the archers. In His side He bore,
> And in His hands and feet, the cruel scars.
> With gentle force soliciting the darts
> He drew them forth, and healed, and bade me live.

For some months more he remained with Dr Cotton,
> 'Whose humanity sheds rays
> That makes superior skill his second praise.'[2]

---

[1] *William Cowper*, Hugh I'Anson Faussett, Cape, 1928, p. 76.
[2] Cowper's 'Hope'.

## God's Mysterious Way

He was now, as for the rest of his life, being kept by his friends and relations, who had clubbed together. He never had any head for business, and one way and another caused them a lot of trouble. Not being able to face a return to professional life, when he left St Albans he wanted to retire to the country, and at first went to Huntingdon to be within reach of his brother who was a don at Cambridge. The loneliness of his life began to tell on him, until he became friends with a family of Unwins, father, mother, son and daughter. He was constantly in their home and before long became a lodger. Mrs. Unwin, though only seven years older, gave him the kind of maternal love his nature needed. She was a peacable, sensible, sympathetic, cheerful person, and, not least important, she shared Cowper's intense evangelical faith. He was really 'at home' for the first time since he was six. He was now thirty-three.

After two years Mr Unwin was killed by a fall from his horse. Cowper still remained a member of the household but they soon decided to move to Olney in Buckinghamshire to be near a dynamic and unconventional parson called Newton, who was curate there for the absentee rector. In Olney Cowper and Mary Unwin were to live for the next twenty years, and Newton became his most intimate and life-long friend.

John Newton's life-story reads like an improbable adventure tale for boys. He lost his mother at the age of six, and was a source of distress and puzzlement to a stiff and unsympathetic, though well-meaning and not unkindly, father. He was a most unreliable youth, throwing away by his slackness several opportunities arranged for by his father. The lack of proper home life was a serious handicap. He went to sea with his father at the age of eleven, was 'pressed' into the Navy at sixteen and became a midshipman. For trying to desert he was flogged and lost his rank, a bitter experience. Rejecting all his early religious training, he became an aggressive atheist who delighted in shocking people by his blasphemous curses. He took service in a slave ship, and became himself practically a slave in the house of a negro woman who grossly ill-treated him. Rescued from there and at sea again, he was converted by reading Thomas à Kempis and enduring a terrible spell of storm in which his damaged ship drifted for nearly a month in privation and danger: food and water were almost exhausted and the crew expected from day to day that the battered and leaky ship might founder on the high seas. For six years he was himself captain of a slave ship, cherishing his new-found Christian faith to the best of his ability, and apparently without any scruples about his ugly trade—though he later became an abolitionist and took an effective part in the support of his friend Wilberforce.

Having to leave the sea through ill health he became 'tide surveyor' at Liverpool, which meant searching ships for contraband. This post allowed him a good deal of leisure. Though he had had little formal schooling he was studious by nature and used his time to good purpose for wide reading and study of Greek, Latin, literature and history. He was greatly impressed by reading Philip Doddridge's life of Colonel Gardiner, killed at the battle of Prestonpans, whose story was not unlike his own. Both had rejected their early faith and fallen into bad ways, and had found their way back again painfully to Christian discipleship. He told a friend that this book 'has affected me more frequently and sensibly than all the books I ever read'.

A man of wide travel and considerable experience at sea as seaman, mate and master, he now wanted to find a place of Christian service. He did much lay preaching in dissenting chapels and felt called to enter the ministry, though for long he was undecided to which Church he should offer himself. Eventually he turned to the Church of England, which showed no eagerness to have him, but after many efforts he secured ordination at the age of thirty-nine and exchanged his comparatively well-paid post for the poverty of the curacy at Olney. Later he became rector of St Mary Woolnoth, beside the Mansion House in London. Here his down-right preaching and warm heart attracted many humble folk to the church, rather to the annoyance of the wealthy merchants living over their counting houses, who were his real parishioners and found their accustomed pews occupied by strangers. He never lost his bluff sailor ways, but with them he had great native ability and a genial manner which won him many friends.

He became an influential and much sought after man, but never allowed himself to forget his past. Over the mantelpiece of his London study he had painted in large letters: 'Thou shalt remember that thou wast a bondman in the land of Egypt, and the Lord thy God redeemed thee.' He composed his own epitaph: 'John Newton, clerk, once an infidel and a libertine, a servant of slaves in Africa, was by the rich mercy of our Lord and Saviour

Jesus Christ, preserved, restored, pardoned, and appointed to preach the Faith he had long laboured to destroy."[1]

This remarkable man played a large part in Cowper's life. At Olney they lived in each other's company and shared long walks together almost daily. Cowper helped in all the work of the parish, as a kind of lay curate. He spoke and led in prayer at the meetings in the Great Hall, which the evangelical Lord Dartmouth had given to Newton as a parish hall. He taught in the Sunday School. He visited the poor and acted as distributor of funds for their relief. It was at Newton's suggestion that he set to work to compose hymns for a book they agreed to produce together. To most of us today these hymns are better known than *The Task*, the poem which made Cowper famous. As a general rule the great poets have not been hymn writers, as Montgomery pointed out.[2] It has been suggested that Cowper and Robert Bridges are the only two in English literature who have won fame in both capacities. It is an interesting judgment, though an arguable one. Certainly by the verdict of their contemporaries, whatever we may think, both Isaac Watts and James Montgomery won laurels in both fields.

Cowper had produced sixty-eight hymns, several of them written earlier, when another attack of his mental trouble brought his writing to a stop. For a while Newton put the project on one side but eventually published the book with 280 of his own in it. *Olney Hymns* appeared in 1779 and had a wide sale both in Britain and America, for private reading and church purposes. We shall not be far out if we think of it as a volume of 'Gospel hymns' for use in mission services. No doubt the authors had their eyes on a wider circle but in the first instance they were aiming at the weeknight meetings in the hall at Olney. It is very unlikely that Newton had any intention of using it in his church. Hymn singing was then doubtfully legal in the Church of England and was certainly frowned on in Prayer Book services, though several collections for local use were beginning to appear.[3]

It has been asserted that Cowper's hymns are full of gloom and reveal a tortured spirit, thus bearing out the cruelty of Newton in making him write them, as some of the biographies will have it. Cowper's madness and its cause is discussed at some length later, but this charge can be dealt with now. One cannot,

---

[1] An excellent detailed account of his life, based on wide research, will be found in *John Newton: A Biography*, by Bernard Martin, Heinemann, 1950. [2] See page 92. [3] See pp. 90ff.

of course, always be confident in equating the 'I' of any hymn writer with himself. He is not always writing autobiography but composing hymns for use by a congregation. This is naturally particularly true of Scripture paraphrases where the writer is mainly concerned to express the thought of the Bible. But there are some hymns which seem clearly to be an expression of Cowper's own mind. A careful analysis of the whole sixty-eight reveals that in fact only a very few show signs of strain and gloom. Most of them are indeed uninspired and unimpressive. One or two not in common use today are striking but so dated in phraseology as to be unsuitable for congregational worship. In the familiar ones we have his best.

So when Mr Faussett judges the hymns as a whole to be poor stuff, we can agree, but not when he goes on to accuse them of 'morbidity', 'dangerous introspection', and even of 'insincerity'. Such a judgment is just fantastic, though it may be noted that Mr Faussett has no use for religion at all, accuses Cowper of insincerity whenever he mentions the subject, and probably regards any reference to sin as being in itself morbid. Only eight of the total are open to the charge of being unhealthily introspective or morbid, and eight out of sixty-eight is not a large proportion. A much larger number express gratitude, confidence and cheerfulness. Stopford Brooke, again, is being much too sweeping when he compares 'the quiet and sober religion of (Watts') hymns' with 'the impassioned and storm-tossed religion of the hymns of Cowper'.[1] Very few indeed merit such adjectives. Many are just dull and pedestrian.

It must in fact be confessed that for the most part Cowper's attempts to translate evangelical doctrine into verse for the simple folk of the Great House meetings just do not come off, though they would probably have a much greater appeal then than now. Like Watts, Cowper was no doubt trying to write down to the level of his audience and leaving out 'the ornaments of Poesy'. Most of his hymns are today completely unknown except to the student and are not in any of our books. Yet eight or ten attain the very highest class by any standard and seem destined to live as long as the English language survives. Wordsworth said poetry should be 'the spontaneous overflow of powerful feeling'. Add intense conviction and you are near to a description of the

---

[1] *Theology in the English Poets*, Everyman Edition, p. 9.

## God's Mysterious Way

best of Cowper's hymns. At least seven are widely used in our churches today.

His greatest are 'Hark my soul', 'Sometimes a light surprises', and 'God moves in a mysterious way'. It would be hard to arrange these in any order of merit.

'Hark my soul' was written at Huntingdon before he met Newton, and is full of Cowper's own experience of deliverance at St Albans. Lord Selborne judged it to be his best and Gladstone rated it as one of the three greatest hymns in the language. Many thousands have sung it as giving expression to their own story, but Cowper was thinking of that great day at Dr Cotton's house. 'We can hardly hear the words without picturing Cowper's radiant face as he joined whole-heartedly in the singing at the Great House.'[1]

> I delivered thee when bound,
> And when bleeding healed thy wound;
> Sought thee wand'ring, set thee right,
> Turned thy darkness into light.

In his *Treasury of Sacred Song* Palgrave describes 'Sometimes a light surprises' as 'a brilliant lyric'. It certainly is, and its trustful faith is no less impressive than its poetic grace. This hymn well illustrates the use of Scripture which is characteristic of Cowper's hymns as a whole. Verse 1 recalls Malachi 4.2 and II Samuel 23.4; verses 2 and 3 Matthew 6 and verse 4 Habakkuk 3.17. Yet the hymn is no laborious piecing together of texts; they are woven into a fabric of beauty and power.

Another that surely belongs to great poetry as well as to great religion is 'God moves in a mysterious way'. It is full of perplexity and awe, yet of confidence too. There is no basis for the story that it was written after his frustrated attempt at suicide in 1773: it was in fact written before that date. Dr Moffatt, in the *Handbook to the Church Hymnary*, calls it, with justice, 'a profound hymn', and it has been described as the greatest hymn on divine providence. *The Oxford Dictionary of Quotations* gives

---

[1] Martin, op. cit., p. 258. How *can* Dr Routley say that Cowper 'was never sure of his salvation; he could remember no conversion'? *Hymns and Human Life*, p. 76f. He knew better when he wrote his earlier book, *I'll Praise My Maker*, where he writes: 'Cowper's experience of conversion was, as we have said, vivid' (p. 67), a statement which he elaborates. But then Routley surprisingly joins in the witch hunt against 'Newton's calvinism'. He seems to me to show here less than his usual insight.

six from this hymn, covering nearly the whole of it. Here indeed are memorable lines.

It is related that the Rev Richard Knill in 1844 gave C. H. Spurgeon, aged ten, a sixpence for learning it and made the boy promise that when he preached in Surrey Chapel, then one of the great shrines of nonconformity, he would give out this hymn. Spurgeon described his emotion when the time actually came for him to keep his promise.

No less established in common use are 'Jesus, where'er Thy people meet' and 'O for a closer walk with God'. The former with 'Heal us, Immanuel', which is in only half as many hymn books, has few rivals in voicing the hopes and aspirations of Christians as they meet for worship anywhere, but they were both peculiarly appropriate to the meeting at Olney. 'Jesus, where'er Thy people meet' was specially written for the day when the little gathering moved into a new and larger hall. A verse in the original directly referred to this event.

There has been a good deal of argument as to whether 'O for a closer walk with God' is really suitable for use in public worship. Ellerton, himself one of our best hymn writers, urged that it was not. 'True and beautiful as it is, it belongs not merely to a secret, but to an exceptional condition of heart; it is plainly impossible that it could be real for a whole congregation at once, even on the hypothesis that the whole congregation were living and faithful Christians. Only a few at any one time would be in the spiritual state indicated in the hymn, and therefore while to the few its value would be great, to the majority it would be unmeaning and thus unfit to offer to God.' The warning against using unreal hymns and inviting people to lay claim to depths of Christian experience to which they are strangers is much needed. But the fact that this hymn is included in all eight of the most used books in this country seems to suggest that the general judgment is against Ellerton, so far as this hymn is concerned. Is this not at least how a worshipping congregation *ought* to be feeling and what many Christians know in their own experience? Is this not a proper mood of aspiration? It is not an easy point to decide.

Controversy also rages round 'There is a fountain filled with blood'. It is included among his best even by those who feel it is unsuitable for public worship. The unpleasant and unbiblical language seems more appropriate to Mithraism with its blood bath than to Christianity. Cowper relies on putting together

## God's Mysterious Way

Zechariah 13.1 and Revelation 1.5, but this imagery is not the New Testament way of speaking of the death of Christ. Yet Norman Nicholson in his study of Cowper protests that 'if this hymn is in bad taste then Christianity itself is in bad taste'. He calls it 'a superb hymn and a remarkable expression of evangelical piety at its purest' (p. 79). While Saintsbury declares that 'No finical or Philistine dislike of the phraseology ought to blind any lover of poetry to the wonderful tranced adoration of the movement'.[1] All the same, it is better kept for private reading.

'The Spirit breathes upon the Word' perhaps also has a reminiscence of the power of the Bible in Cowper's own experience at St Albans. It is still in wide use today.

Only the *Methodist Hymn Book* preserves that lovely poem 'Ere God had built the mountains' though Garret Horder[2] rates it as 'his grandest hymn'. It is a paraphrase of Wisdom 7.22-31.

This time at Olney was probably the happiest period of his life, yet it is possible that this concentration on religious activities was not very wise for such as Cowper. His kindly cousin Harriet, now Lady Hesketh, was not a particularly religious person and may perhaps have been a little irritated by his excess of zeal, and on both accounts somewhat biassed, but one cannot help feeling some sympathy with her comment in a letter to Theodora: 'Mr Newton is an excellent man, I make no doubt, and to a strong-minded man like himself might have been of great use: but to such a mind . . . such a tender mind, and to such a wounded yet lively imagination as our cousin's, I am persuaded that eternal praying and preaching were too much.' Perhaps he was relying on his emotions and keeping himself too tightly keyed up. His religious feelings were bound to cool off after a time and when Cowper began to lose his first zest he wondered if this meant that he was falling from grace. Just at this point came the shock of the death of his brother John. The precariously balanced nervous system was set trembling once more and eventually gave way. His melancholia was not essentially religious but expressed itself in his over-strained mind in religious imagery and he came to believe that God had pronounced on him sentence of damnation. Of course, to recognize an element of truth in the charge that too much emotional religion was bad for him is quite a different

---
[1] *History of English Prosody*, II, p. 533.
[2] *The Hymn Lover*, p. 125.

matter from admitting that his hallucination was caused by anything in the teaching of Newton, or any other evangelical.[1]

Mrs Unwin gave herself completely to looking after him, at great cost to her own health. 'He held on to Mrs Unwin's hand like a child in the dark'.[2] Newton generously took them both into his own house and did all he could to help. After about two years Cowper began to emerge from his darkness. He began to do odd jobs of cleaning and carpentry about the house. The hares, Bess, Puss and Tiny, given him by neighbours, brought him a new interest in feeding them, taming them, and studying their ways. A dog, a cat, birds, all joined the household. Best of all, he took up gardening.

But wise Mary Unwin saw that the time had come when his mind too needed to be more exercised and at her suggestion he began again to write poetry, in which he had dabbled during his London days. At first, as Mr Nicholson says, he took up poetry 'merely to occupy his mind, as convalescents take up knitting or jig-saws' (p. 44), but latent gifts appeared and he began really to work at it. So at the age of forty-nine he embarked seriously on a career of authorship. It was a very late hour to be starting. Poetry, for the most part, comes to the young. Wordsworth was twenty-eight and Coleridge twenty-six when *Lyrical Ballads* appeared, and Tennyson had published much of his best before he was thirty-three. Shelley and Keats were even younger. A quiet, busy routine developed until he had produced a whole book of verse, published in 1782 as *Table Talk*. It was not a very good book and created little stir, though it would be wrong to write it off as a failure, and at least its writing had done much to save the author. At last he had a job to do that really absorbed him.

Newton had gone off to London, followed by Cowper's intimate

---

[1] I am glad to find that Norman Nicholson, in what I regard as the most sensitive and understanding of recent books on Cowper, though that of Gilbert Thomas belongs in the same class, shares this judgment: 'There seems no doubt whatever that (Newton) led Cowper into a most exacting life of piety, prayer meetings, public charity and private self-denial, which was far too severe for the poet's nervous system. Yet I find it very hard to believe that it was from his teaching or influence that Cowper derived the obsession with damnation which was to bring so much horror into his later years,' *William Cowper*, Lehmann, 1951, p. 40. This charge will be examined more closely later.

[2] David Cecil, *The Stricken Deer*, p. 148.

and affectionate letters. But a great friendship had now developed with William Bull, the Congregational minister at Newport Pagnell, *carissimus taurorum*, 'most beloved of bulls', a man of some learning, imagination and humour, and altogether a most congenial companion, though inseparable from a pipe, which did not please Cowper nearly so well! Another who now came into his life had even more exhilarating effects, the vivacious Lady Austin. Mary, William and she became the closest of friends and the rather sedate household was much enlivened. It was she who told him the story that became 'The Diverting History of John Gilpin', one of the best bits of humorous verse in English. It was she, too, who started him off on *The Task*. But when it became clear that Lady Austin cherished hopes of a closer relationship than her pretended sisterhood, both William and Mary were alarmed. Cowper had to break off the friendship, greatly to his grief, but partly also, I suspect, to his relief.

*The Task*, published in 1785, was a triumphant success which put its author at once among the leading poets of the age. It rambles through a host of topics, politics, social questions, gardening, religion. The eighteenth century found it good reading, and so can we. 'God made the country and man made the town' comes from here and might almost serve as its text. He wrote to a friend that the poem 'as a whole has one tendency, to discountenance the modern enthusiasm after a London life, and to recommend rural ease and leisure, as friendly to the cause of piety and virtue'. It starts off with mock heroics on a sofa, but has the reader out of doors with little delay, and into the real country which Cowper knew and loved, not the artificial scenery of groves peopled by nymphs, swains and shepherdesses, which was the stock-in-trade of contemporary poetry. 'My descriptions are all from nature—not one of them second-handed. My delineations of the heart are from my own experience; not one of them borrowed from books or in the least conjectural.' Birds, animals, country folk and country ways are accurately and lovingly observed and recorded. He was not in the least sentimental about it. He knew all about muddy roads, damp in the house, slush, and he was familiar with the extreme poverty of many of the people, with drunkenness and squalor.

Fashionable London read *The Task* with avidity for its gay wit and fresh descriptions of nature, and found themselves confronted with its serious message. For Cowper puts his wit and vigour at the service of social reform and takes a wide sweep over debtors' prisons, the Bastille, then still standing, blood sports and cruelty to animals, the government of India, gambling, slavery, the behaviour of the clergy, and a host of other topics. He has something to say of the soldier, the statesman, the lawyer, the man of fashion, and the parson, as well as of the poor in their near-by cottages. He is passionate in his denunciations of slavery, cruelty and war. He has his epigrams and sayings that have passed into our common speech: 'God made the country and man made the town', we have already met; 'England, with all thy faults, I love thee still'; 'variety's the very spice of life'; 'Cups that cheer but not inebriate'; 'He is the freeman whom the truth makes free'; 'I am monarch of all I survey'; 'Riches have wings'. *The Oxford Dictionary of Quotations* devotes twelve columns to Cowper.

Leslie Stephen says that Cowper knew too little of the world's affairs to be able to produce pointed satire. 'His tone and feeling too frequently suggests the querulous comments of old ladies gossiping about the outside world over their tea-cups, easily scandalized by very simple things' (p. 209). Or as Mr Nicholson puts it, 'when he takes it on himself to make denunciations of the great—of courtiers, statesmen and the like, his words are as shrill and hollow as those of the president of the village Mothers' Union condemning the night life of London' (p. 49). This is clever but not altogether just. Insistence on Cowper's ignorance of 'real life' can be overdone. After all he was a barrister and had lived in chambers for twelve years as one of a gay company of young literary gentlemen, among 'beaux, wits, poets, critics and every character in the gay world', in his own words, and had rather prided himself on his dress and society manners. His family was one of real standing in the national life. He cannot have kept eyes and ears tight shut. We have to admit that there are at times traces of a narrow outlook, as in his silly attack on science in the Third Book, but many of his comments on affairs are well-informed and pointed.

His deliberate moralizing does not appeal to everybody but it is all very readable. He is at times perhaps more of a preacher in verse than a lyric poet, though he has his times of high inspiration. 'My sole drift is to be useful, a point however which I know I should in vain aim at unless I could likewise be entertaining,' he writes to Lady Hesketh. Or in another letter, 'My readers will hardly have begun to laugh before they will be called upon to correct their levity to peruse me with a more serious air.' All in all, without doubt he was the most popular poet of his day and exercised an immense influence. Many of his shorter poems also are imperishable parts of English literature; such varied pieces as 'Alexander Selkirk', 'The Loss of the Royal George', 'John Gilpin', 'Boadicea', 'The Flatting Mill', 'To Mary', 'Yardley Oak', which is not so much a parable from nature of the growth and decay of human like, but even more the story of a tree for its own sake. Cowper was leading the way to a new kind of poetry, new both in style and in subject. He put his thoughts in natural words in their natural order, breaking with the formalism and artificiality of Pope and his kin. He is moved by the love of nature and of his fellow men, and finds both in the presence of God. He has set his feet on a path which Wordsworth and Burns were to tread, though the former was only fifteen when *The Task* appeared, heralding the romantic revival.

Perhaps Cowper's letters would qualify him for literary immortality even if there were no hymns and no poetry. The best letters in English, said Southey; certainly there is nothing of the kind more delightful. Never intended for publication, they were dashed off to reflect the mood and interests and requests of the moment; 'the divine chit-chat of Cowper,' as Coleridge called them. They picture life in the home and the village and are full of narrative, kindly gossip and humour, just as it comes. It is only rarely that they contain for his intimate friends the outpouring of his miseries too. Several times in the letters he rather preens himself on his isolation and detachment from all public affairs, but that is only the prelude to some searching comment on the political issue of the moment. In spite of his disclaimer he did indeed follow the course of events with keen interest, as poems and letters both show. It is most tempting to linger among them and to indulge in many quotations. They are a joy to read and reread. I must be content to add my testimony to that of those who hail Cowper as one of the greatest of letter writers. 'Cowper's letters,' said Wordsworth, 'are everything that letters can be.'[1]

But we must return to Cowper, bereft of the lively but alarming Lady Austin. Fortunately another visitor saved the situation, his

---

[1] Knight's *Life of Wordsworth*, III, p. 376.

cousin Harriet, full of kindness and cheerfulness, bringing unobtrusive financial help, including the provision of a much more comfortable home at Weston. Two months after the move, however, in 1786, Mary's son and Cowper's friend, William Unwin, died of typhus after a week's illness, leaving a young wife and two small children. It was a severe shock to them both and brought to Cowper a third attack of madness, this time of shorter duration and with an apparent recovery.

But greater disasters still were in store. In 1788 Mary Unwin herself had a 'stroke', followed by a second in 1791, and was completely incapacitated until her death in 1796. She became unable to do anything unaided, to cross the room, to feed herself, to knit or to read, and her mind became affected. Cowper gave up everything to nurse her, including his writing and the country walks that had meant so much. 'She has been my faithful and affectionate nurse for many years, and consequently has a claim on all my attentions. She has them and will have them as long as she wants them.' The well-known and most moving poem, 'My Mary', tells the story. When Mary died in December, 1796, she was buried secretly at night to spare him the funeral. Not surprisingly Cowper was physically and mentally overwhelmed by the strain and his obsession with the belief that God had forsaken him persisted. For four more years he dragged on his existence, until he died in 'unutterable despair', in his own words, at East Dereham, Norfolk, on April 25th, 1800.

His last poem, 'The Castaway', is based on a tale he had read in Anson's *Voyages* of a sailor washed overboard who drowned in sight of his would-be rescuers.

> No voice divine the storm allayed,
> No light propitious shone,
> When snatched from all effectual aid,
> We perished, each alone:
> But I beneath a rougher sea,
> And whelmed in deeper gulfs than he.

Cecil sees this as the final outburst of Cowper's 'accumulated anguish and despair'. But one cannot help wondering, with Goldwin Smith, whether utter despair really expresses itself in a polished work of art. One would not for a moment wish to gloss over the tragedy of it all, but to get a true picture of Cowper's life it is necessary to remember that most of the time he was sane and cheerful and that his attacks, dreadful though they were, came at long intervals. All his principal poems and his most lively letters were written after the attack of 1773. His poetry shows little or no trace of his mental instability. Even when he writes gloomily his words are not always to be taken at their face value. In even the gloomiest of the letters there are glints of the most delightful wit. He was a man of moods and they alternated with great rapidity.

It is now time, and perhaps more than time, to face squarely the issues that have inevitably kept on emerging: was Cowper's madness due to his religious faith, and was Newton responsible for his collapse; these are, of course, two questions, not one. For it has become the fashion among Cowper's biographers, with one or two notable exceptions, to blame everything on 'Newton's calvinism' and his 'inhuman God', in Mr Faussett's phrase. And some of those who acquit religion of the blame are still convinced that Newton was guilty. What evidence is there?

It is really disheartening to discover how frequently these bogeys of 'calvinism' or 'evangelicalism', or even 'puritanism' are paraded in several studies of Cowper, with very little indication that the writers have any knowledge of their real nature and teachings. They are often ignorantly used as synonyms for narrow-mindedness and a harsh, gloomy outlook on life. Personally I repudiate the doctrines of extreme or 'hyper' calvinism and dissent heartily from much of the teaching of eighteenth century evangelicalism, but I equally resent their sweeping condemnation by those who seem to have taken little trouble to understand them. And it is certainly fantastic to lay upon its shoulders the blame for all that went wrong with Cowper. I say 'its', but in truth calvinism and evangelicalism are far from being synonymous, though some of the critics do not distinguish between them. Wesley, the leader of the evangelical movement, was an arminian and spent all his life denouncing calvinism.[1]

It will help to clear the air to recognize, in the first place, that Cowper's illness was of a type familiar to modern medicine and one that has no necessary connection with religion at all. In a recent volume an eminent psychiatrist, Dr E. B. Strauss, describes the symptoms of a 'depressive psychosis' as follows: 'Depression, difficulty in concentration, loss of interest in every-

[1] See p. 52.

thing, finding everything, especially routine activities, an effort; insomnia with early waking; loss of weight; flatulent dyspepsia; diminution of sexual appetite and performance; self-reproach and self-depreciation, with irrational guilt feelings, tearfulness, suicidal impulses, retardation, fatiguability, irritability.'[1] A psychosis he defines as 'a psychic disorder in which the psyche, regarded analogically as a piece of structure, is temporarily or permanently damaged (there is a *lesion* of the psychic structure) and in which insight is *apt* to be impaired but by no means always' (p. 28). By insight he means awareness of the irrational nature of the symptoms. The trouble is frequently recurrent and such cases often grow in 'a crescendo of misery and despair'. Treatment by modern methods, often by electric shock,[2] is frequently successful—'in eighty or ninety per cent of cases'.

We have not, of course, got a medical report on Cowper, but much data is available, and so far as the general picture is concerned it seems to a layman in these matters that Dr Strauss might be giving a description of Cowper's own case. And could anything have been more likely to produce 'a lesion of the psychic structure' than Cowper's experiences in early childhood, to which reference has been made. It may be added that hallucination and 'voices' are not uncommon in this type of mental illness, and Cowper was convinced he had heard the voice of God speaking directly to him in a nightmare in February, 1773, pronouncing judgment, curiously enough in Latin: *actum est de te, periisti*, said the voice. 'It is all over with thee, thou art lost.'

Again, it must be noted that, so far from 'calvinism' causing his madness, the first attack came before he had any noticeable religion at all, certainly before his conversion to evangelicalism, and before he had even heard of Newton. Indeed it was his conversion which temporarily cured him, or coincided with his cure, and led to the happiest and sanest period of his life, lasting several years. We might truthfully add that evangelicalism kindled his poetic flame and kept it burning, even after his first emotional

[1]*Psychiatry in the Modern World*, Michael Jospeh, p. 50.
[2]One is astonished to come on this passage in Bull's *Life of John Newton* with reference to Cowper: 'It may also be added that it occurred to Mr Newton to try on his friend the effect of the electrical shock, and this he did but without any salutary result. We have mentioned these facts', including the calling in of Dr Cotton again, 'because it is thought in some quarters that Mr Newton did not at once use all the means that might have been tried for Mr Cowper's recovery' (p. 187).

## God's Mysterious Way

enthusiasms had calmed down; even, astonishing as it may seem, after he had come to believe that while redemption was not available for him, it was available for others.

The most vigorous statement of the charge against both religion and Newton is that of Mr Faussett. At the outset of his book he speaks of 'those instinctive fears which an evangelicism' (so he persists in calling it) 'tainted with calvinism, was later so disastrously to excite' (p. 21). 'If his nerves could have been spared the strain which was now' (under Newton at Olney) 'imposed upon them by evangelical enthusiasm, he might have in time adapted his faith to the rational as well as the emotional needs of his nature, and so never acquired, through a return of madness, the delusion which was to darken the rest of his days—that he was abandoned by the God he had failed to propitiate' (p. 91). 'To this tragic delusion Cowper was brought by a fatalistic religion. For it was a false theology that bound his despair to his mind with knots which no restoration of spirits could untie' (p. 127).

If it is possible to attach the word theology to the fancies of Cowper's delirium, it was indeed a false theology. But if Mr Faussett means that Cowper had learned this theology from Newton, or any other exponent of evangelical Christianity, he must produce his evidence. It is poles asunder from anything Newton believed or taught. I like, for example, the robust common sense and steady faith of this letter from Newton to Cowper in one of his times of depression. 'How strange that your judgment should be clouded on one point only, and that on a point so obvious and strikingly clear to everybody who knows you! How strange that (you should think that God) could ever forsake and cut off the soul which He has taught to love Him! . . . Though your comforts have been so long suspended, I know not that I ever saw you for a single day since your calamity came upon you in which I could not perceive as clear and satisfactory evidence that the grace of God was with you, as I could in your brighter and happier times. In the midst of all the little amusements which you call trifling, and which I would be very thankful you can attend to in your present circumstances, it is easy to see who has your heart, and what way your desires tend, as to see your shadow when you stand in the sun' (May 6th, 1780).

Calvin's fundamental concern was to teach the absolute sovereignty of God and the complete dependence of man in his sin on God's grace and goodness. That is essential Christianity. But Calvin believed that this involved, in the light of the mysterious facts of life, a doctrine of double predestination, and it is this that the critics no doubt have in mind. God, Calvin held, has appointed some to salvation and some to damnation. He shows His mercy in saving the elect and His justice in condemning the reprobate and it is presumptuous to ask why some are saved and others not: the marvel is that any at all should be saved. Calvin did not invent this doctrine, which was propounded also by Augustine and Aquinas. It is completely logical *if one accepts the premises,* but the premises from which it starts are un-Christian. Calvin's premise is that God is sovereign and inscrutable will, but we know God in Christ as redeeming love, and 'it is surely a supreme example of bad logic to deduce a Divine resolve to condemn certain souls to ruin prior even to their existence, from the character of a Christlike heavenly Father'.[1] All Christians declare with gratitude that our salvation does not depend on human merit but on the grace of God, but we have no right to declare that He has rejected any as outside salvation, rather the contrary.

We do not know what Cowper believed in this respect, but it does not really bear on his trouble, as the critics appear to think. For Cowper had been taught, and knew that he had been taught, that a man once brought to Christ would never be allowed finally to be lost to Him. For we must note this further in calvinistic doctrine: faith is the result, not the cause, of our election. If we have faith, if we are once in communion with Christ, we have evidence of His 'effectual calling' of us. And there can be no danger of anyone who has once so entered into fellowship with God falling away from grace. In believing that he had been rejected after having been once accepted, Cowper was *not* following calvinistic teaching. He was in fact denying the calvinistic doctrine of the perseverance of the saints. Cowper admitted that he had been taught to believe this, but declared, in spite of calvinism, that he was an exception to the rule, 'The dealings of God with me', he wrote to Newton in July, 1786, 'are to myself utterly unintelligible. I have never met either in books or in conversation with an experience at all similar to my own.'

---

[1] H. R. Mackintosh, *The Christian Apprehension of God*, SCM Press, p. 223.

At another time he writes: 'My friends, I know, expect that I shall see yet again. They think it necessary to the existence of divine truth that he who once had possession of it should never finally lose it. I admit the solidity of this reasoning in every case but my own. And why not in my own? For causes which to them it appears madness to allege, but which rest upon my mind with a weight of immovable conviction.' So one must not blame his obsession on Newton or on what he had been taught as evangelical doctrine, which is what Mr Faussett and others assert.

I can find no evidence that Newton preached extreme predestinarian doctrines and much to the contrary. Such a verse as this might have been written by the arminian Charles Wesley:

> Approach, my soul, the mercy seat
>   Where Jesus answers prayer;
> There humbly fall before His feet
>   For none can perish there.

Nor does the hymn by which Newton is best known suggest the preaching of a God of terrors:

> How sweet the name of Jesus sounds
>   In a believer's ear!
> It soothes his sorrows, heals his wounds,
>   And drives away his fear.
> It makes the wounded spirit whole
>   And calms the troubled breast.
> Tis manna to the hungry soul
>   And to the weary rest.

If only Cowper had given heed to that!

Newton was in fact a very moderate calvinist and always under suspicion by his more orthodox brethren. 'I find,' he complained, half jokingly, 'that I am considered as an Arminian among the high Calvinists and as a Calvinist among the strenuous Arminians.' If calvinism is the steady, cheerful, though not starry-eyed, faith of Newton's hymns it could never have produced Cowper's morbid introspection and torture of heart. In them, as Gilbert Thomas says, 'there is far more of love than of fear' (p.222). Does this not unrepresentative stanza sound like 'grim calvinism'?

> O sinners, hear His gracious call.
>   His mercy's door stands open wide!
> He has enough to feed you all,
>   And none who comes shall be denied.

It passes my comprehension how anyone who has actually read

Newton's hymns and letters can speak as does a writer in Julian's *Dictionary of Hymnology* of his 'extreme despondency'.

It makes an effective contrast of the general outlook of the two to set side by side what they have to say on a somewhat similar theme, though Cowper's hymn, as demonstrated above, is not a representative one. First take Cowper:

> The billows swell, the winds are high,
> Clouds overcast my wintry sky;
> Out of the depths to Thee I call,
> My fears are great, my strength is small.
>
> Amidst the roaring of the sea
> My soul still hangs her hope on Thee;
> Thy constant love, Thy faithful care,
> Is all that saves me from despair.
>
> Though tempest-tossed and half a wreck
> My Saviour through the floods I seek.
> Let neither winds nor stormy main
> Force back my shattered bark again.

Contrast with this the robust confidence of Newton's well-known hymn:

> Begone, unbelief,
>   My Saviour is near
> And for my relief
>   Will surely appear.
> By prayer let me wrestle,
>   And He will perform;
> With Christ in the vessel
>   I smile at the storm.

It is worth while to quote one more of Newton's hymns, not so well-known, which might have been, and perhaps was, written as an antidote to Cowper's fears:

> Be still, my heart! These anxious cares
> To thee are burdens, thorns and snares.
> They cast dishonour on my Lord
> And contradict His gracious word.
>
> Brought safely by His hand thus far
> Why wilt thou now give place to fear?
> How canst thou want if He provide,
> Or lose thy way with such a guide?
>
> When first before His mercy seat
> Thou didst to Him thy all commit,

> He gave thee warrant from that hour
> To trust His wisdom, love and power.
>
> Did ever trouble yet befall
> And He refuse to hear thy call?
> And has He not His promise past
> That thou shalt overcome at last?
>
> He who has helped me hitherto
> Will help me all my journey through . . .

Cowper gave up the more emotional religion of earlier days, and for a time at least, public worship and private prayer. For him they were meaningless or even sinful, though not for others. Numerous letters could be quoted in illustration of this attitude. Writing to Newton (February 8th, 1783) he says: 'Mrs U. thanks Mrs. N. for her kind letters and for executing her commissions. We truly love you both, think of you often, and one of us prays for you; the other will, when he can pray for himself.' He did not become an atheist. He continued to believe in the existence of God and in His goodness *to other people*. He envied those with steadfast faith and was sure that other believers passed at death into a haven of peace and love. But this was not for him. His despair was inaccessible to argument. He knew *he* was rejected and deserted.

Sometimes the cloud lifted. As illustration of one such time, and to show how little he found Newton a depressing influence, I quote a letter regarding a projected visit to Sussex for the sake of Mary's health. He shrank from it for several reasons and wrote to Newton (July 30th, 1792):

'Once I have been on the point of determining not to go and even since we fixed the day my troubles have been insupportable. But it has been made a matter of much prayer, and at last it has pleased God to satisfy me in some measure that His will corresponds with our purpose and that He will afford us His protection. You, I know, will not be unmindful of us during our absence from home, and will obtain for us, if your prayers can do it, all that we would ask for ourselves, the presence and favour of God, a salutory effect of our journey and a safe return.

'I rejoice, and had reason to do so, in your coming to Weston, for I think the Lord came with you. Not, indeed, to abide with me; not to restore me to that intercourse with Him which I enjoyed twenty years ago; but to awaken in me, however, more spiritual feeling than I have experienced, except in two instances, during all that time. The comforts that I received under your ministry in better days all rushed upon my recollection; and during two or three transient moments seemed to be in a degree renewed. You will tell me that, transient as they were, they were yet evidences of a love that is not so; and I am desirous to believe it.'

To sum up, Cowper was suffering from the hallucinations of madness, not from the doctrines of calvinism or the influence of Newton. 'Cowper's religious terrors were obviously the effect and not the cause of the madness,' wrote Leslie Stephen in the *Dictionary of National Biography*.

Though we may be able to trace some of the causes of Cowper's tragic story, and even to see some light in his darkness, this does little to explain *why* such things should happen to such a man. And we may confess ourselves baffled. Here is an instance of the problem of evil in an acute form, and one hesitates to say anything which may look like an attempt to pass it by with a few pious phrases. Yet something must be said.

Our knowledge of God in Christ authorizes us to assert without hesitation that Cowper was mistaken in his belief in divine desertion, wherever he got it from. We remember that saying of St John: 'If our heart condemn us, God is greater than our heart, and knoweth all things.' The delusions of men do not change the reality of God's love. Mrs Browning has a poem called 'Cowper's Grave', which does not lend itself to quotation but is full of a sympathetic understanding. She reminds us that Christ Himself on the Cross uttered a terrible 'orphaned cry' and that He surely went through that experience that no such words of desolation should be used by those He came to save. And she pictures a boy in the delirium of fever crying out for his mother, not realizing that all the time she is there beside his bed caring for him. And when he wakes from his fever it is to find her still there. So she sees Cowper declaring that God has forsaken him, yet waking from his fevered dream of life to find himself in His presence.

# 5

# STAND UP AND BLESS THE LORD!

*James Montgomery (1771-1854), the layman
who left an imperishable inheritance*

IN his day Montgomery achieved an immense reputation as a poet. The public bought his books and the poets acknowledged him as of their company. Wordsworth, Southey, Scott and Moore all expressed admiration for his work, and he was considered as a possible successor to Southey as Poet Laureate. Byron even went so far as to say, in a footnote to *English Bards and Scotch Reviewers*, that Montgomery's *A Wanderer in Switzerland* (1806) was worth a thousand *Lyrical Ballads* and that its author was 'a man of considerable genius'. That same *Wanderer* achieved nine editions in England and twenty in the United States. Emerson was so impressed by it that he sought out Montgomery when he visited this country in 1848. But at the height of his fame a friend asked him which of his poems he thought would live. 'None, sir,' he replied, 'nothing except perhaps a few of my hymns.' And so it has proved. In the preface to his collected *Original Hymns* he refers to them as 'the most serious work of my long life (now passing four score years)'.

His family were originally Scottish though they had been settled for several generations in Ireland, and it was in Scotland that he was born, at Irvine, in Ayrshire, where his father was minister of the Moravian church, then the only one in Scotland. When he was five his parents moved back to Ireland, to the Moravian settlement at Ballymena, which had been founded in 1764 by John Cennick, himself a hymn-writer of some distinction. In 1783, when James was twelve, his parents went as missionaries to Barbadoes and he was sent to the Moravian School at Fulneck, near Leeds. A disappointment to his teachers, he seemed to be more interested in trying to make verses than in his lessons, and they were more than doubtful if he would ever make a minister, as had been the intention. 'James Montgomery,' say the school records, 'notwithstanding repeated admonitions has not been more attentive. It was resolved to put him to a business, at least for a time.' So at the age of sixteen he was apprenticed to a baker. This was to be the beginning of a period of restless, unhappy years. He ran away from the bakery and found work in a general store at Mirfield. At eighteen he went off to London to try to find a publisher for his poetry but without success, and he returned to the shop counter at Wath, near Rotherham. Both his parents had died in the West Indies before he was twenty.

Then in 1792 he answered an advertisement in the *Sheffield Register* and was appointed clerk and book-keeper to its printer, editor and proprietor, Joseph Gales. He now began to find an outlet for his literary gifts and became a frequent contributor to the paper. So when Gales fled to America two years later, to escape prosecution for articles which the authorities considered seditious and revolutionary, no doubt made extra suspicious because of events in France, Montgomery was made editor. He changed the name to *The Sheffield Iris* and went on editing it for thirty years. Later he became its owner.

Like Gales he was a man of strong radical views and it was not long before he got himself imprisoned twice; in 1795 on account of a poem on the fall of the Bastille, and in the following year for an article criticizing the action of a magistrate in dispersing a riot. In prison he sang, in words reminiscent of Lovelace:

> Blest with freedom unconfined
> Dungeons cannot hold the soul.

His radical views coloured all his later work. He attacked slavery in his poem, 'The West Indies', and actively supported Wilberforce and Clarkson in their crusade. He refused to insert advertisements of state lotteries, declaring them 'a national nuisance'. He took up the cause of the chimney boys before Lord Shaftesbury in his poem, 'The Climbing Boy'. He wrote much poetry and many hymns, and was an active supporter of many religious and philanthropic causes. He never married. Though he retained a life-long connection with the Moravians, for many years he attended a Wesleyan Methodist Church and towards the end of his life became a communicant in the Church of England.

He sold the paper in 1825, but continued writing and speaking, the foreign missionary enterprise, Sunday schools and the Bible Society being three of his main interests. Concerning himself with such varied matters as education, public health, the reform of the police, and the provision of a municipal gas supply, he became a recognized leader in the civic life of Sheffield. In 1835 he was awarded a national pension by Sir Robert Peel. At a banquet in his honour in Sheffield he said: 'I wrote neither to suit the manners, the taste, nor the temper of the age. I sang of war—but it was the war of freedom in which death was preferred to chains; I sang the abolition of slavery; I sang the love of home; I sang the love which man ought to bear towards his brother of every kindred and country and clime upon earth; I sang the love of virtue; I sang too the love of God, who is love.' 'Montgomery was emphatically a good man,' writes Richard Garnett in the *Dictionary of National Biography,* 'greatness whether intellectual or poetical cannot be claimed for him.'

It is interesting to read an account of his personal appearance at the age of seventy, written by Hugh Miller in *The Witness* on the occasion of a visit to Edinburgh. 'His hair has assumed a snowy whiteness . . . but the expression of the countenance is that of middle age. It is a thin, clear, speaking countenance; the features are high; the complexion fresh though not ruddy, and age has failed to pucker either cheek or forehead with a single wrinkle. . . . The figure is quite as little touched by age as the face. It is well but not strongly made, and of the middle size.'

He died on April 30, 1854, in Sheffield where he had lived for sixty-two of his eighty-two years. He was given a public funeral, a statue was erected to his memory, a Wesleyan chapel and a public hall were named after him, and there is a stained glass window in his parish church. A special service was held a year or two ago to commemorate the centenary of his death.[1]

His poetry included 'The West Indies', 1810, to which reference has been made; 'The World Before the Flood,' 1812, an epic on the wars of the giants and the patriarchs, much of it written before he was twenty; 'Greenland', 1819, founded on the Moravian work there, and 'The Pelican Island', 1836. A series of lectures on poetry, praised by the DNB, was delivered in the Royal Institution and published in 1833. His *Collected Poems* were published in 1841. 'On the whole he may be characterized as something less than a genius and something more than a mediocrity,' is Garnett's verdict.

---

[1]There are *Memoirs* in seven volumes, of 'the most formidable prolixity' says DNB, edited by John Holland and James Everett, 1854-6, and a biography by W. King, 1858.

But if he is only a minor poet, he is among the half-dozen greatest hymn-writers in English. He began writing hymns as a schoolboy at Fulneck, in imitation of the old Moravian ones, and he wrote his last the day before he died. In *Songs of Zion,* 1822, he included paraphrases of fifty-six psalms. *The Christian Psalmist,* 1825, is an anthology of hymns, which includes many of his own and a notable introduction at which we shall look more closely later. He wrote some 400 hymns in all, and 355 are included in his *Original Hymns.* On reading them through one is surprised to find that many not in our modern hymn books could be sung in church today just as they are, with entire satisfaction and with no feeling of their being dated. And there are very few collections of old hymns of which that could be said! Some of these are not in our books just because there are now better ones on the same themes; for example, his very attractive rendering of the Twenty-third Psalm, good as it is, cannot compete with our familiar versions. The book contains several notable paraphrases in addition to those we all know.

Many of these hymns are not suitable for use in public worship and were never intended for it, as his sub-title makes clear: 'For public, private and social devotion.' By their very nature several have a personal reference, such as his moving poem, 'For a Deaf Man', or 'For Mariners' or his rather curious dialogue between Christians and Gypsies. Very interesting is his 'Garden Thoughts', inspired by a missionary meeting held in a garden, linking together the gardens of the Bible, impossible to sing but good to read. The volume would still make a welcome and helpful companion for private prayer.

The number of hymns for anniversaries and other special occasions suggests, what was indeed the fact, that Montgomery was regarded as a kind of Christian poet laureate to be approached when churches or societies wanted something written appropriate to an event. His skill, and kindness of heart, was tested by many stone-layings and openings of new chapels. Many were written for the Whitsun Sunday School festivals which were once such a feature of the year. It is said that he wrote a new hymn for the Sheffield Festival each year for nearly forty years. Here too are hymns for the centenary of the Moravian Church and of Wesleyan Methodism, for the jubilees of the Baptist Missionary Society, the Religious Tract Society, and the Church Missionary Society, and for the opening of hospitals in Dublin and Sheffield.

## Stand Up and Bless The Lord! 85

When those wedded to special events are deducted the proportion of the remaining total still in common use becomes all the more impressive. Julian's *Dictionary of Hymnology* says that in 1891 one hundred were in general use. That astonishing figure could not be expected to last, but more recent figures are still noteworthy. *Congregational Praise* contains 22 of Montgomery's hymns, *Church Hymnary* 15, *Baptist Hymn Book* 14, *Methodist Hymn Book* 14, *Hymns Ancient and Modern*, 1950, 11, *B.B.C. Hymn Book* 11, *English Hymnal* 10, and *Songs of Praise* 8.

With few exceptions the hymns are carefully constructed, the thought consecutively followed through and the whole bound into a unity, often by the skilful repetition of a key phrase. This is strikingly seen in 'Songs of praise the angels sang', where that phrase occurs at a different point in each verse. Other instances are 'Stand up and bless the Lord' and 'Angels from the realms of glory'. And ever and again there comes a memorable phrase with that 'inevitability' which is one of the marks of true poetry. Characteristic of his style is the frequent use of the exclamation, or of the imperative in which often members of the congregation appear to be exhorting each other. In unskilful hands these are dangerous practices, but Montgomery seldom fails with them. Illustrations are 'Hail to the Lord's Anointed!' 'Hark the song of jubilee!', 'Baptize the nations!', 'Stand up and bless the Lord!', 'Lift up your heads, ye gates of brass!', 'Sow in the morn thy seed!'.

His hymns are objective, strong, bracing, uplifting, with hardly a trace of morbid introspection anywhere in the collection. There are some of penitence and heart-searching, but for the most part they bid men look to God in Christ; it is the Christian facts and events they emphasize rather than the psychology of the soul. The range of subjects is wide. There are hymns for the great festivals and on the life of Christ on earth. Several are on the Bible, many on prayer, and numbers are admirably expressive of the spirit of worship. His strong missionary interest keeps appearing; indeed his outlook is ecumenical, in hailing and celebrating 'the holy Church throughout all the world', and in his care for its unity. And he does not forget the beauties and terrors of nature. Garrett Horder, the distinguished student of hymns, justly declared that 'for variety, clearness, strength, suitability of form to subject, (they) have rarely, if ever, been excelled'.[1] Julian's verdict is worth

[1] *The Hymn Lover*, p. 158.

quoting not only for its justice but also for the Victorian rotundity of its phraseology; 'richly poetic without exuberance, dogmatic without uncharitableness, tender without sentimentality, elaborate without diffusiveness, richly musical without apparent effort.'

Dr Routley calls him 'the greatest of Christian lay hymn writers'. The statement makes one think. If one takes into account both the quality and the quantity of the hymns which are in use today the judgment is probably correct. But it all depends on what one means by 'greatest'. Montgomery faces considerable competition and certainly greater poets than he are among our lay hymn writers, and many who achieved greater fame in other fields. There are Cowper, Bridges and Addison, Kipling and Chesterton, John Milton and William Blake, and Thomas Carlyle. It is interesting also to recall the names of other laymen who have made a notable contribution to our hymns, though they do not rank with those we have just listed: Ebenezer Elliott, Oliver Wendell Holmes, John Byrom, Bowring, Palgrave, W. C. Dix, Thomas Hughes and Josiah Conder, who was a notable pioneer hymn book editor and author of six hymns to be found in *Congregational Praise*. And that is not all. If women are to be taken into account there would be nearly as many names to add, for they have made a great contribution. To mention only one or two out of a noble company, there are Christina Rossetti, Cecil Frances Alexander, Catherine Winkworth, and that outstanding pioneer, Anne Steele.[1] It is good to be reminded how many lay folk have had a memorable share in the great work of hymn making. But reflection shows that all told Routley is right, with the possible exception of William Cowper.

Confining attention now to the eight current hymn books, I find that between them they include twenty-nine hymns by Montgomery. Two appear in all eight. 'Hail to the Lord's Anointed', an 'imitation of Psalm 72', as he called it, is a hymn of triumphant faith. He first recited it at the end of a speech at a missionary meeting in Liverpool, and it is easy to believe that the audience was thrilled. The original last line read, 'His name, what is it? Love', which he later changed to 'That name to us is love.' Keble is said to have been responsible for the alteration to 'His changeless name of Love', which appeared in *Hymns Ancient and*

---

[1] See further, chapter 10, p. 126.

## Stand Up and Bless The Lord!

*Modern* in 1861 and has been adopted in many books.

Equally widely used is his other great missionary hymn, 'Lift up your heads, ye gates of brass'. The original title of this, in nineteen verses, was 'China Evangelized' and instead of the now usual 'To Christ shall all the nations bow' Montgomery wrote, 'To Christ shall Buddha's votaries bow'. 'Hark the song of jubilee', popular in the Free Churches, is in none of the Anglican collections. And only three books use that other fine missionary prayer-hymn, 'O Spirit of the living God'.

One of his most interesting hymns in this field had almost completely dropped out of use, but is being happily revived by *Congregational Praise*, 'Within Thy courts have millions met'. Its theme is interestingly similar to that of the better known, 'The day Thou gavest', though I am not aware of any evidence that Ellerton found his inspiration here. It is so good and so little known that I quote some of the ten verses, as they are in his *Original Hymns*.

> Millions within Thy courts have met,
>    Millions this day before Thee bowed;
> Their faces Zionward were set,
>    Vows with their lips to Thee they vowed.
> People of many a tribe and tongue,
>    Men of strange colours, climates, lands,
> Have heard Thy truth, Thy glory sung,
>    And offered prayer with holy hands.
> Still, as the light of morning broke
>    O'er island, continent or deep,
> Thy far-spread family awoke,
>    Sabbath all through the world to keep.
> From east to west, the sun surveyed,
>    From north to south, adoring throngs,
> And still where evening stretched her shade
>    The stars came out to hear their songs.
> And not a prayer, a tear, or sigh,
>    Hath failed this day some suit to gain;
> To those in trouble Thou wert nigh,
>    Not one hath sought Thy face in vain.
> Yet one prayer more?—and be it one
>    In which both heaven and earth accord;
> Fulfil Thy promise to Thy Son,
>    Let all that breathe call Jesus Lord.

'Angels from the realms of glory' finds a place in seven books. It first appeared in Montgomery's paper, *The Sheffield Iris*, on Christmas Eve, 1816. He summons in turn the angels, the shepherds, the magi, and the expectant in Israel, like Simeon, to worship the new born King. His last verse has been omitted from most modern books.

> Sinners, wrung with true repentance,
> Doomed for guilt to endless pains,
> Justice now revokes her sentence,
> Mercy calls you—break your chains,
> Come and worship
> Worship Christ, the new born King.

*Songs of Praise*, followed by *Hymns Ancient and Modern*, 1950, has happily substituted another, taken from a carol by another writer in *The Christmas Box* of 1825,

> Though an infant now we view him
> He shall fill His Father's throne,
> Gather all the nations to Him;
> Every knee shall then bow down.

Four of the books use another of his Christmas hymns, 'Songs of praise the angels sang', poetically one of his best, looking forward from the songs of the angel choir at Bethlehem to the triumphant songs of heaven. The future life is also the theme of one of his most widely used hymns, 'For ever with the Lord', which is in six books. His original contains twenty-two verses, and is better suited for private reading, even in the shortened version, than, despite its popularity, for public worship.

'According to Thy gracious word', in seven books, is a widely known Communion hymn, showing deep devotional feeling movingly expressed. Another admirable hymn for the Lord's Supper has only two verses, which no doubt has prevented its wide adoption; it is in only two books. In America it is said to have won its way with the addition of other verses, beginning 'Shepherd of souls', from an untraced source. In this form it is in the *Baptist Hymn Book* in this country.

> Be known to us in breaking bread,
> But do not then depart;
> Saviour, abide with us, and spread
> Thy table in our heart.

## Stand Up and Bless The Lord!

> There sup with us in love divine;
> Thy body and Thy blood,
> That living bread, that heavenly wine,
> Be our immortal food.

Six collections contain his rousing call to worship, 'Stand up and bless the Lord'. Montgomery is at his happiest in hymns of worship, though not many appear in modern hymn books, no doubt because there are such rich stores for editors to draw upon. Other worship hymns of his in one or two books are 'Holy, holy, holy, Lord', 'Command Thy blessing from above', 'To Thy temple I repair', and 'Glad was my heart to hear'.

One of Montgomery's most famous compositions, which is in six hymn books, and often appears in devotional anthologies, is 'Prayer is the soul's sincere desire'. More a devotional poem than a hymn, it is an instance of his poetic gifts at their best. He said he had received more messages as to its helpfulness than about anything else he had written. He wrote many others on prayer but only one is in any number of our modern collections, 'Lord, teach us how to pray aright'.

A favourite for services of ordination and induction, and for ministers' meetings generally, is 'Pour out Thy Spirit from on high', which finds a place in seven of our books, in two of them with an altered first line, 'Lord, pour Thy Spirit'. Four books use the Whitsun hymn, 'Lord God the Holy Ghost'. Only three have his bracing, confident hymn, 'God is my strong salvation', based on the Twenty-seventh Psalm, which is deserving of much wider use.

> God is my strong salvation;
> What foe have I to fear?
> In darkness and temptation
> My light, my help, is near.
>
> Though hosts encamp against me,
> Firm to the fight I stand;
> What terror can confound me,
> With God at my right hand?
>
> Place on the Lord reliance;
> My soul, with courage wait;
> His truth be thine affiance
> When faint and desolate.
>
> His might thine heart shall strengthen,
> His love thy joy increase;

Mercy thy days shall lengthen;
The Lord will give thee peace.

The other Montgomery hymns still in use in these British books can only be named: 'Sow in the morn thy seed', 'Go to dark Gethsemane', 'This stone to Thee in faith we lay', 'In the hour of trial', 'Jesu, our best beloved friend', 'O God, Thou art my God alone', and 'Palms of glory'.

But Montgomery's influence on hymnody was not confined to the hymns he wrote himself. We ought not, for example, to pass by his share in a controversy which played a great part in opening the door to the general use of hymns in the Church of England. Many Anglicans were distressed to see the practice of hymn singing spreading from parish to parish accompanied by a positive rash of books. According to Julian (p. 333f) and Benson (p.353) at least fifty hymn books for Anglican use were published between 1800 and 1820. Ellerton[1] speaks of 'a fashionable watering place' (meaning probably Brighton where he had been curate) which a few years ago, he is writing in 1864, had twelve different hymn books in use in its fifteen churches, six or seven of them being peculiar to the congregation in which they were in use. The then Bishop of Peterborough declared that the hymn book was often regarded as more important than the Prayer Book. It was feared that hymn books would be vulgar and lack taste, for it was well known that the whole business originated with the dissenters and that only the extreme evangelicals in the Church of England had taken it up. There was a danger of their teaching false and unchurchly doctrine. Some even declared that the very practice of hymn singing was contrary to the laws of the Church of England; nothing was authorized but the Old Version of the Psalms, or Sternhold and Hopkins, and the New Version, or Tate and Brady. Some bishops sought to prohibit the use of hymns altogether.

The issue came to a head with the prosecution of Thomas Cotterill: and this is where Montgomery became involved. Thomas Cotterill, 1779-1823, was a close friend of Henry Martyn at Cambridge where they both came under the influence of Charles Simeon. In 1817 he came to St Paul's Church, Sheffield, after work in the Potteries. For use in his former parish at Lane End in Staffordshire he had compiled a hymn book of 170 hymns.

---

[1]Housman, p. 206.

## Stand Up and Bless The Lord! 91

Seven editions of this had been sold before he went to Sheffield. Naturally he introduced its use in his new parish. This roused great opposition on the part of many in the congregation. They declared that his book had no authorization and that in any case hymn singing in church was illegal. On these grounds they denounced Cotterill to the Consistory Court of York. But Archbishop Harcourt was sympathetic with Cotterill's purposes, and proposed a way out. He suggested that Cotterill should withdraw his unauthorized book and prepare another to be submitted to himself for authorization. Montgomery was already a distinguished poet and a fellow citizen, and Cotterill appealed for his help. Together they compiled a new collection, to which Montgomery contributed eleven of his own hymns, and the Archbishop gave it his official sanction, and indeed supplied the Sheffield church with copies inscribed, 'The gift of his Grace the Archbishop of York'. The book became a model for several successors, and the whole affair gave publicity and encouragement to the cause of hymn singing in general and did much to overcome Anglican prejudices. Cotterill and Montgomery were kindred spirits and became close friends, and Montgomery was greatly distressed when Cotterill died in 1823, after only six years in Sheffield. It was then that Montgomery wrote his poem reprinted in his *Original Hymns,* 'Friend after friend departs'.

Montgomery was also our first English hymnologist of any note: he collected hymns and discussed the fundamental principles of their content and style. In *The Christian Psalmist,* 1825, he brought together 562, including a number by himself, but with many by Watts, the Wesleys, Doddridge, Newton, Ken, Cowper, Heber, Addison, and several others, still known or forgotten. Some come from Moravian sources and from the two pioneers, Anne Steele, who has six, and twenty-two from Benjamin Beddome, for whom he expressed great admiration. The book is rather an anthology of verse of the hymn type than a book for use in public worship, for which much of the contents is obviously unsuitable. But with the collection itself I am not here concerned.

It is in the prefaces to this volume and to his edition of *Olney Hymns* that Montgomery's reflections on hymnology are to be found. Since they are not readily accessible an outline of their contents may be of interest. In the 'Introductory Essay' of *The Christian Psalmist,* running to twenty-eight pages, he calls attention to the fact that the great poets have seldom written hymns;

indeed Cowper is 'the only great poet of our country' who has written any number. This is partly due to the fact that many eminent poets have not been Christians. But it is partly due to 'the idle prejudice', fostered by Dr Johnson in his lives of Watts and Waller, that sacred subjects are unfit for poetic treatment. This Montgomery vigorously challenges. 'Had our greatest poets possessed the religious knowledge of our humbler writers of hymns, they might have been the authors of similar compositions, not less superior to the ordinary run of these, than their own best poems are above the incorrigible mediocrity of their contemporaries'. Even without their aid, this collection of his, he claims, provides proof that 'hymns may be as splendid in poetry as they are fervent in devotion'. 'A hymn ought to be as regular in its structure as any other poem; it should have a distinct subject, and that subject should be simple, not complicated, so that whatever skill or labour might be required in the author to develop his plan, there should be little or none required on the part of the reader to understand it. . . . There should be a manifest gradation in the thoughts, and their mutual dependence should be so perceptible that they could not be transposed without injuring the unity of the piece.' Every part should be subservient to the unity of the whole. Too many hymn writers, he complains, produce a series of disconnected thoughts driven by the exigencies of rhyming. You could leave out bits, or alter the order of the verses, without any loss. That is not the way to construct a true hymn. Too often 'the meanness of the workmanship is dishonouring to the grandeur of the theme'. 'Authors who devote their talents to the glory of God and the salvation of men ought surely to take as much pains to polish and perfect their offerings of this kind, as secular and profane poets bestow upon their works.'

Montgomery then proceeds to comment upon the compositions of several of the most notable of the writers in his collection. Of Bishop Ken's three hymns he says, 'Had he endowed three hospitals, he might have been less a benefactor to posterity. There is exemplary plainness of speech, manly vigour of thought, and consecration of heart in these three pieces.' 'The greatest name among hymn writers' is that of Dr Isaac Watts. In his hymns 'he has embraced a compass and variety of subjects which include and illustrate every truth of revelation, and throw light upon every secret movement of the human heart, whether of sin, nature or grace, and describe every kind of trial, temptation, conflict, doubt, fear, and grief, as well as the faith, hope, charity, the love, joy, peace, labour and patience of the Christian in all stages of his course on earth, together with the terrors of the Lord, the glories of the Redeemer, and the comforts of the Holy Spirit, to urge, allure and strengthen him by the way'. 'Dr Watts may almost be called the inventor of hymns in our language'. Few of his hymns resemble those of his predecessors and he has established a model for all successors. Montgomery commends his catholic outlook, so that you could not discover from his hymns to which denomination he belonged. And he rejoices that these hymns are sung every Sunday by many thousands throughout the world, and that some of them will live 'as long as the language of Britain endures'. There are inevitably many flaws in them, such as occasional prosaic phraseology and bad rhymes, which have had an unhappy influence on his imitators, 'for while his faults and defects are most faithfully adopted, his merits are unapproachable'.

'Next to Dr Watts as a hymn writer undoubtedly stands the Rev Charles Wesley.' Like Watts he covers the whole range of Christian experience 'with an affluence of diction and a splendour of colouring rarely surpassed. At the same time he has invested them with a power of truth and endeared them both to the imagination and the affections with a pathos which makes feeling conviction, and leaves the understanding little to do but to acquiesce in the decisions of the heart.'

Addison's four hymns are 'very pleasing. . . . It is only to be regretted that they are not more in number, and that the God of grace as well as the God of providence is not more distinctly recognized in them.' Doddridge's hymns may be frequently deficient in poetry but are 'lovely and acceptable . . . for that fervent unaffected love of God, His service and His people which distinguishes them'. There are references to Moravian hymnody, to Cowper, Newton and Toplady. It is worth pausing on his reference to the Baptist, Benjamin Beddome, not only as doing honour to a great pioneer, now mostly forgotten, but also because what he says throws light on Montgomery himself. Beddome's compositions, he writes, 'are calculated to be far more useful than attractive, though on closer acquaintance they become very agreeable as well as impressive'. Each contains 'a single idea, always important, often striking, sometimes ingeniously brought out . . . with the terseness and simplicity of the Greek epigram'. 'His name would deserve to be held in everlasting remembrance if he had left no other memorial of the excellent spirit which was in him than the few humble verses:

> Let party names no more
> The Christian world o'erspread;
> Gentile and Jew and bond and free,
> Are one in Christ their Head.
> Among the saints on earth
> Let mutual love be found;
> Heirs of the same inheritance,
> With mutual blessings crowned.
> Let envy and ill will
> Be banished far away,
> And all in Christian bonds unite,
> Who the same Lord obey.
> Then will the Church below
> Resemble that above.
> Where no discordant sounds are heard,
> But all is peace and love.'

In his introduction to an edition of *Olney Hymns*, dated January, 1829, Montgomery deals almost entirely with Newton, having previously edited an edition of Cowper's *Poems*. *Olney Hymns* 'has become a standard book of its kind among devout readers of every evangelical denomination'. Newton's is much the larger part 'and it is no disparagement of his memory to say that this might be considerably reduced with advantage to the remainder'. He repeats his earlier claim that while 'hymn writing, like every other kind of poetry, has a style suitable to itself', a real poet will do the job better than a mere versifier. 'The major necessarily includes the minor capacity'. Cowper shows the 'perspicuity, simplicity and ease' which Newton, 'his less gifted coadjutor', declares are needed in hymns, but combines them with 'grace, elegance, pathos and energy, such as poetic inspiration alone could supply'.

As he closes the Essay in *The Christian Psalmist* Montgomery declares that 'if he knows his own heart', 'he would rather be the anonymous author of a few hymns which should become an imperishable inheritance to the people of God, than bequeath another epic poem to the world, which should rank his name with Homer, Virgil, and our greater Milton'. His prayer has been heard. He has left to us 'an imperishable inheritance'.

# 6

# IN EVERY PART WITH PRAISE
## *Horatius Bonar (1808-89),*
## *the prince of Scottish hymn-writers*

THE man whom Dr James Moffatt called 'the prince of Scottish hymn writers', and who still holds an unrivalled place in his own country and one of great prominence in the hymnody of all English speaking lands, was born in Edinburgh in 1808, the son of a solicitor. The family had given a succession of ministers to the Church of Scotland since 1693 and Horatius had two brothers who were known, like himself, as great preachers and influential leaders in the life of parish, Church and nation. He was educated at the Edinburgh High School and University, where he was a pupil in the theological classes of the great Thomas Chalmers, and achieved distinction as a classical and theological student. His first appointment was as assistant to a church in Leith where he was engaged in mission work among a very rough population. In 1837 he was called to be parish minister in Kelso in the Scottish Borders.

When the Disruption came in 1843 he followed Chalmers out of the Church of Scotland into the new Free Church. Because they believed that the government was interfering with the spiritual freedom of the Church, mainly in relation to 'patronage' and the intrusion of ministers into parishes against the wishes of the parishioners, some four hundred ministers and many more laymen, led by the Moderator, walked out of the Church Assembly to constitute themselves into a new Church in another building, electing Thomas Chalmers as their first Moderator. This heroic decision meant that the dissenters were giving up all claim to the funds and properties of the Church of Scotland; congregations left the buildings where they and their forefathers had worshipped and ministers gave up their manses and salaries to step into the unknown. Nearly a third of all the ministers and people seceded. In a few years, through sacrificial giving and labours, the new Church had created a complete national organization of churches, schools, colleges, and foreign missions. Happily the breach is now mended and 1929 saw a reunited Church.

Bonar himself stayed on in Kelso as minister of a new Free Church until in 1866 he became minister of the Chalmers Memorial Church in Edinburgh. In 1883 he was appointed Moderator of the Free Church General Assembly, the highest honour his Church could confer. He was a man of tireless energy, expressed in many forms of service, and a voluminous writer. Some of his then famous series of 'Kelso Tracts' and devotional books had a very large circulation. It is said that 285,000 copies of his book, *God's Way of Peace*, were sold. He often visited London and was a regular speaker at the Mildmay Park Conferences. When a young man he was much impressed by Edward Irving and made the Second Advent of Christ a prominent feature of his ministry. For twenty-five years he edited a quarterly *Journal of Prophecy,* including a hymn of his own in each number.

He began to write hymns very early and published several volumes of them. They achieved immense popularity in his lifetime, and about fifty years ago it was estimated that as many as a hundred were in regular use. Even today thirty are to be found in one or more of the standard British books. When he began his ministry hymns were not used in the regular services of his Church, but he found that the continual use of the metrical Psalms made little appeal to the young people in Leith. So he wrote hymns for them to be sung to lively popular tunes. 'I lay my sins on Jesus', 'I was a wandering sheep', and 'A few more years shall roll' are said to have been his first. His experience encouraged him to go on. Altogether he wrote over six hundred hymns. He used to carry a note book everywhere, and at odd moments he would enter in it ideas for hymns, phrases, lines. He was a careless writer and published too hastily without proper revision. In the introduction to a collection of them published after his death his son said, 'He was not concerned about small imperfections in the structure of his verse, if the verse carried his message.' That message was warmly evangelical, one of hope through the love of God for His children. Though sympathetic he is never sentimental, and in spite of the carelessness there is often a note of real poetry. He could have achieved a much higher literary standard if he had been prepared to give time to reconsideration and polishing. His range of vision was limited, but he speaks with deep sincerity of what he knows. *Hymns of Faith and Hope* was the title he gave to a series of volumes. In the first he said: 'They belong to no Church or sect. They are not the expression of one man's or one party's faith and hope: but are meant to speak what may be thought and spoken by all to whom the Church's ancient faith and hope are dear.'

It is characteristic of the man's work as a whole that his two most widely used hymns today should be one of evangelism and one for the Lord's Supper. 'I heard the voice of Jesus say' is in all the books and is surely a model for such hymns: 'Here, O my Lord, I see Thee face to face', also in all the books, is one of the most familiar and helpful for use at the Holy Communion. Next in general use, though curiously not in the *Church Hymnary*, is 'Fill Thou my life, O Lord my God, In every part with praise', a prayer that the whole of life may be lived in fellowship with God. 'Go, labour on' was written to encourage the workers in his church at Leith. Equally popular, rather surprisingly, is 'Thy way not mine, O Lord', which is much less happily constructed and less effective than his other well-known hymns. Five books also contain 'Beloved, let us love', a masterpiece of condensed and meaningful writing, summing up the teaching of the First Epistle of John.

The hymn which Bonar himself liked best of his own writings is in only three books, 'When the weary seeking rest', based on II Chronicles 6.29ff. 'Light of the world, for ever ever shining' has more of real poetry than many of his: there is a haunting quality about the words. Probably the first hymn he wrote for the young folk at Leith was 'I lay my sins on Jesus'. He said of it himself that it was good Gospel but not good poetry, and it does not seem a very suitable hymn for children, whatever its merits for others. One of his best seems little known, and the selection of verses in the *Church Hymnary* is not the happiest, to my thinking. His text might be 'Herein is love, not that we loved God but that He loved us'.     Not what I am, O Lord, but what Thou art,
>  That, that alone, can be my soul's true rest.

The thought is worked out in skilful and helpful fashion. Another, on the same theme, is also too little known.

> Not what these hands have done
> Can save this guilty soul;
> Not what this toiling flesh has borne
> Can make my spirit whole.

> Not what I feel or do
> Can give me peace with God;
> Not all my prayers and sighs and tears
> Can bear my heavy load.
>
> Thy love to me, O Lord,
> Not mine, O Lord, to Thee,
> Can rid me of this dark unrest
> And set my spirit free.

Full of his favourite subject is 'O Love of God, how strong and true' which one would expect and wish to find in more than five books. It is worth quoting somewhat fully for its own sake, because it is not widely known, and because it is the heart of what its author was trying to say all his life.

> O Love of God, how strong and true!
> Eternal and yet ever new;
> Uncomprehended and unbought,
> Beyond all knowledge and all thought.
>
> O heavenly love, how precious still
> In days of weariness and ill,
> In nights of pain and helplessness,
> To heal, to comfort, and to bless!
>
> O wide embracing, wondrous love,
> We read thee in the sky above;
> We read thee in the earth below,
> In seas that swell and streams that flow.
>
> We read thee best in Him who came
> To bear for us the Cross of shame,
> Sent by the Father from on high,
> Our life to live, our death to die.
>
> We read thy power to bless and save
> E'en in the darkness of the grave;
> Still more in Resurrection light
> We read the fulness of thy might.
>
> O love of God, our shield and stay
> Through all the perils of our way;
> Eternal love, in thee we rest,
> For ever safe, for ever blest!

If that can be given as the summing up of his message, then the spirit of his long service in the Christian ministry is expressed in a hymn eminently suitable for use at meetings of ministers or in their private devotions. Yet unhappily only one hymn book contains it. I quote one or two of its many verses.

> We thank Thee, Lord for using us
>   For Thee to work and speak;
> However trembling is the hand,
>   The voice however weak.
>
> For solace ministered perchance
>   In days of grief and pain;
> For peace to troubled, weary souls,
>   Not spoken all in vain.
>
> Lord, keep us still the same as in
>   Remembered days of old;
> O keep us fervent still in love,
>   Mid many waxing cold.
>
> Help us, O Christ, to grasp each truth
>   With hand as firm and true
> As when we clasped it first to heart,
>   A treasure fresh and new.
>
> O honour higher, truer far,
>   Than earthly fame could bring,
> Thus to be used, in work like this,
>   So long, by such a King!

# 7

## THE ROYAL BANNERS

*John Mason Neale (1818-66)
and the hymns of the Catholic Revival*

IF Pusey is to be believed, and few can have been in a better position to know, the Oxford Movement, which deeply affected English hymnody, actually had its birth if not in hymns at least in poems. He traced its real source to the publication in 1827 of Keble's *The Christian Year*. Issued anonymously at first, this is not a hymn book but a series of meditations, 'Thoughts in Verse for the Sundays and Holy Days throughout the year', in the words of its sub-title. The message of the Oxford Movement does not lie on the surface of the book: indeed Hurrell Froude feared it might be attributed to a Methodist! But the charm of its poetry threw a new glamour over the liturgical celebrations of the Church's Year, and over the whole course of religious observance commanded in the *Book of Common Prayer*. It prepared men's minds for what the Movement had to say. Though not written as hymns, and mostly quite unsuitable for such use, extracts from its poems have become some of our best known and best loved hymns; in particular, 'Sun of my soul', 'There is a book', and 'New every morning is the love'. And beyond doubt one of the most lasting, and on the whole beneficent, effects of the Movement was on our hymnody. In this field, as in others, all sections and denominations of the Church gained much, even those to whom some aspects of its message were most repugnant.

The Church of England was then badly in need of a stimulant. Its vitality was at a low ebb and the bishops were particularly unpopular, partly because of their stubborn opposition to the Reform Bills. So grim was the general outlook that Thomas Arnold could write in 1832, 'The Church as it now stands no human power can save.' His remedy was to relax what he regarded as its too rigid credal demands, to give the laity a larger part in its government, to regulate the powers of the episcopate, and to bring Church and Dissent together into a new national Protestant federation, excluding Unitarians and Roman Catholics. His views were largely shared by Maurice, Kingsley and Stanley, and were formulated in a pamphlet, *Principles of Church Reform*. But neither the Church of England nor the nonconformists responded. The attraction of his scheme for the Dissenters was perhaps not increased when he advocated it on the ground that it would be 'a means of modifying their fanaticism and dissociating them from the utter coarseness and deformity of their chapels!'[1] It was in fact from an almost opposite direction that salvation came.

Whatever weight should be attached to Pusey's judgment about *The Christian Year* no one will dispute the volcanic effect of Keble's Assize Sermon in the university pulpit at Oxford on Sunday, July 14, 1833. His subject was 'National Apostasy' and his immediate concern the Bill then before Parliament for the abolition of ten Irish bishoprics, in which Keble saw the beginnings of a plan for despoiling the Church of England and interfering with its spiritual prerogatives. And the Church itself he regarded as being in a condition of disloyalty and decay.

The sermon brought together a group of men who determined to fight in defence of the Church, its Prayer Book, and the apostolic succession of its ministry. This group organized largely supported petitions to Archbishop Howley. In September of the same year, apparently independently but with the same objectives, Newman launched the first of the historic series of *Tracts for the Times*, from which the Movement got its name of Tractarian. He was supported by Keble and Froude, and after some hesitation by Pusey. The adherence of Edward Pusey was of great significance. Regius Professor of Hebrew in the University and Canon of Christ Church, he was a man of standing, and came with Keble and Newman to form the triumvirate of the Movement, another of whose nicknames thus came to be 'the Puseyites'. The Tracts were announced as being 'against Popery and Dissent'. Their object was to recall the Church of England to its high calling as a divine institution and not a state establishment, as a trustee of the Catholic Faith with roots going far back before the Reformation, and with a ministry descending in an unbroken line from the apostles.

[1] Op. cit., 4th edition, p. 99, quoted by H. R. T. Brandreth, in *History of the Ecumenical Movement*, edited by Rouse and Neill, p. 275.

The Movement rapidly gathered strength and won many enthusiastic supporters, and a host of no less violent opponents among Broad Churchmen and Evangelicals alike, who feared for the Ark of the Covenant. Some of its supporters, stung by the stubborn resistance of the Church as a whole, thought the logic of their movement pointed them to Rome, and to Rome they went, thus confirming the suspicions of their evangelical opponents. W. G. Ward, F. W. Faber, and Frederick Oakeley became Romans, followed in 1845 by Newman himself, after some miserable years of hesitation. At last he had made up his mind that the Church of England was neither catholic nor apostolic. Scholar, poet, and writer of brilliant prose, he was a bewildered genius who never found either himself or his home: 'an angel who had lost his way.' Ward had published a Rome-ward looking book on *The Ideal of a Christian Church* which was censured by the Heads of the Oxford Colleges, while Pusey was suspended from preaching to the university for two years in consequence of a sermon on the Eucharist. The Romeward drift went on. In 1850 others went over, including R. Wilberforce and Manning, like Newman on his way to a Cardinal's hat. From 1850-70 the Movement had to endure much bitter opposition and ridicule, but its influence, for good and for ill, spread throughout the entire Church of England, and far beyond. This is not the place to attempt a general assessment. Our concern here is principally with its profound influence on hymnody, which in turn is one of the greatest influences in the life of any Church.

One of the aims of the Movement was to bring about a much-needed reform in standards of reverence and dignity in public worship, a concern much more fundamental than the comparative details of vestments and ritual which obsessed some of its disciples. Inevitably its attention was directed to hymns, then mainly a preserve of the evangelicals, so far as the Church of England was concerned. Much of the propaganda of the Movement was done through the medium of religious verse. Keble's *Christian Year* had an immense vogue and sold 108,000 copies in twenty-five years. In 1833 he joined with Newman, Froude, Isaac Williams and others in *Lyra Apostolica* containing poems more aggressively 'catholic' than those in the *Christian Year*. Various liturgical investigations were set on foot in furtherance of the

## The Royal Banners

general aim of restoring all possible links with the pre-Reformation Church.

John Chandler thought he had found something they were all seeking when he discovered the *Paris Breviary*, and in 1837 he published *The Hymns of the Primitive Church, now first collected, translated and arranged*. Unhappily these hymns were not at all 'primitive' but contemporary with Isaac Watts! Chandler's gifts as a translator could not alter the fact that the *Paris Breviary* had been issued in 1736 and that its hymns were mainly the work of a group of French poets with the avowed intention of replacing ancient hymns by up-to-date ones. A similar work published the same year by Bishop Mant, *Ancient Hymns from the Roman Breviary*, again contained hymns introduced to meet modern taste by Pope Urban VIII in 1632. The way to antiquity seemed hard! But it had at least been established that so far from being a nonconformist or evangelical intrusion into Christian worship, hymns had been an integral part of the Roman Daily Office and of the Mass itself from ancient times. Hymns were truly 'catholic' after all, and when the genuine pre-Reformation hymnody was discovered it brought a great enrichment, though the enthusiasm of the Tractarians took them too far. They wanted hymns which should be statements of doctrine rather than reflections of personal experience, the voice 'not of the individual believer but of the worshipping Church'.[1] 'Church hymns,' said Neale, in the introduction to *Hymns of the Eastern Church*, 'must be the life-expression of all hearts'; they should not be too intimate or express the experience of the exceptional mystic. But the wholly desirable recovery of emphasis on the great events of the Christian Year and on the Church itself, led also to the commemoration in a host of flat and unconvincing hymns of many very minor events and little known saints and martyrs, from which even the admirable 1950 edition of *Hymns Ancient and Modern* has not fully recovered.

Several of the leaders of the Oxford Movement made notable contributions to hymnody, through both translations and original writing. To John Keble (1792-1866) reference has already been made. Newman (1801-90) is known by only two hymns, though of superlative quality, the rather enigmatic 'Lead, kindly light', which even its author in later years could not or would not interpret,

---

[1] Benson, *The English Hymn*, p. 498.

and the magnificent 'Praise to the Holiest in the height' from his *Dream of Gerontius*. A verse in this hymn has been frequently charged, without any justification that I can see, with teaching transubstantiation. No doubt Newman believed in that doctrine, but what he is declaring here is the reality of the Incarnation, God Himself manifest in the flesh, in Person and not only through the gifts of His grace.

> And that a higher gift than grace
>   Should flesh and blood refine,—
> God's presence and His very self,
>   And essence all divine.

But what a pity that the hymn tails off into such a feeble ending. Is that really all that Newman had to say as the sum of the matter:

> Should teach His brethren, and inspire
> To suffer and to die?

Some of the hymns of F. W. Faber (1814-63) also touch the heights, and some the very bottom of sentimental bathos. *Olney Hymns* had 'acted like a spell' upon him, he said. 'Even Catholics can be found poring with an unsuspecting delight over the Olney Hymns.' He wanted to provide a Catholic alternative, free from the evangelical taint.[1] Among Faber's great hymns are 'O God, Thy power is wonderful', 'Souls of men' (often beginning in hymn books as 'Was there ever kindest shepherd'), 'Sweet Saviour, bless us ere we go', 'O come and mourn with me a while', and 'O it is hard to work for God'. Some of his hymns had to be pruned of assertive Romanism before they could be usable in other Churches, but the fault of many is a sentimentalism that makes them too sweet for healthy appetites. How his meaningless rhythm 'Hark, hark, my soul' is tolerated at all, I cannot imagine. But there is much in his work for which to be grateful.

Like Faber and Newman, Frederick Oakeley (1802-80) left the Anglican ministry for the Church of Rome. His greatest contribution to our hymns is his translation of *Adeste fideles*, 'O come, all ye faithful'. A Fellow of Balliol and a leader of the Oxford Movement, when vicar of All Saints', Margaret Street, he was suspended by the Bishop of London for his extreme ritualism, and resigned his Anglican orders. As a Roman Catholic priest he

---

[1] It is significant that Neale's biographer should refer to this Anglican work as 'the Olney Methodist hymn book'!

worked among the poor of Westminster and was made a Canon of Westminster Cathedral.

Richard Mant (1776-1848), Bishop in the Church of Ireland, to whose collection of 'ancient' hymns reference has been made, is known today by two of his own: 'Round the Lord in glory seated' (or 'Bright the vision that delighted') and 'Saviour, who exalted high'.

Isaac Williams (1802-65) wrote three of the Tracts and contributed to *Lyra Apostolica*. He was an unsuccessful candidate for the professorship of poetry at Oxford on Keble's retirement, the opposition being largely based on his authorship of Tract LXXX, 'On Reserve in Communicating Religious Knowledge'. He wrote and translated many hymns which are now little used, though eight are in the most recent edition of *Hymns Ancient and Modern*, and one or two may be found in other books. He was Newman's curate at St Mary's, Oxford, but did not follow him to Rome.

Edward Caswall (1814-78) was an intimate friend of Newman and after he had himself become a Roman priest joined him at the Oratory of St Philip Neri in Birmingham. He greatly enriched hymnody, especially by his translations of Latin hymns, published in *Lyra Catholica* and other volumes. We are indebted to him for, among others, 'O Jesu, King most wonderful', 'Jesus, the very thought of Thee', 'When morning gilds the skies', 'The sun is sinking fast', 'See amid the winter snow', and 'Come, Thou Holy Spirit'.

But far outreaching all these in the extent of his influence in hymnody was John Mason Neale (1818-66). Julian rightly describes it as 'enormous'. Drawn into the Oxford Movement as a student at Cambridge, he stood up for its principles all through his too brief life, and at great personal cost. It is amusing to see in his letters how he uses the word 'catholic' to mean all that is good and venerable, while 'protestant' is a synonym for unworthy. He even describes a beautiful oak wood as 'catholic'. It is a relief to find his daughter calling attention to the fact that he was on very friendly personal terms with many dissenters! A brilliant classic and of great intellectual ability generally, he had to be content with a pass degree, because honours in classics could then only be attained by one who had previously taken the mathematical tripos. This Neale found quite beyond him, though his father had actually been Senior Wrangler. (This regulation was rescinded the year after he had taken his degree.) But he won the Seatonian Prize for poems on religious subjects eleven times and became a Fellow of Downing.

Lung trouble made it impossible for him to remain vicar of Crawley: he was only in the parish for six weeks. The doctors told him the only chance of prolonging his life was to spend the winters in a warmer climate, so for three years he wintered in Madeira, returning to England for the summers. The doctors then pronounced him cured, and he had no further serious illness until the end of his life. He made good use of his enforced leisure for study and writing: he and his wife occupied a small villa in the hills above Funchal, and he began there his notable *History of the Holy Eastern Church*, his greatest scholarly work, left uncompleted at his death, though several volumes had been published. He was delighted to find an excellent library in Madeira, at the Seminary, to which he was given freedom of access.

Neale had an absorbing interest in anything to do with churches, their structure, architecture, decoration and liturgy. He felt this was an aspect too much neglected by the earlier Tractarians who were concerned mainly with doctrine and order. When at Cambridge he founded in 1839 the Cambridge Camden Society, later called the Ecclesiological Society. Its members set themselves to accumulate masses of detailed replies to an elaborate questionary about churches—any churches anywhere, attractive or unattractive, old or new, great cathedrals or obscure village buildings. Neale spent his holidays 'taking' churches, as he called it. He travelled widely in Western Europe as well as all over England and Scotland, as far as the Orkneys, though he was never able to visit Eastern Europe where his greatest interests lay. The Society gathered a large membership and included many distinguished names. It had a great influence in securing the improvement or restoration of churches and its advice was sought from all over the British Isles and indeed from all over the Anglican Communion.

In 1846 Neale became Warden of a home for old people, Sackville College, East Grinstead, Sussex, a striking quadrangled Jacobean building, standing on high ground with magnificent views over Ashdown Forest and the Downs. It must in those days have been rather like the Hiram's Hospital of Trollope's Barchester novels. This was his home for twenty years, until the end of his life. At the age of twenty-eight he undertook the care of some twelve aged septuagenarian male pensioners and about the same number of old women. It was a surprising task, but he got very fond of his charges whom he served devotedly, though some of them gave him a lot of trouble. He lived in the College and received a minute salary of some £28 a year. The buildings had been neglected and he set himself to restore them in co-operation with the patron, Lord De La Warr. His particular care was the chapel and this led to his first troubles.

A neighbouring evangelical parson visited the College one day and was horrified to find a Cross and candlesticks on the altar. Routing around he discovered a breviary in Neale's own seat—which he did not in fact use in the chapel but had happened to leave there. The visitor jumped to the worst conclusions and wrote to the Bishop to denounce this flagrant 'popery'. The result was that though the College chapel was not under episcopal jurisdiction, Bishop Gilbert, without giving any reasons, inhibited Neale from officiating as priest anywhere in his diocese. Appeals to the Bishop by Lord De La Warr and Neale had no effect. In one letter Neale gave him the assurance, which is amply borne out by all the evidence, that 'there is no man in the whole Church of England more faithful to her than I am; no one to whom it would be more impossible to desert her for Rome'.[1] ('Deserters' was Neale's invariable term for those who seceded to Rome.) The inhibition, much to Neale's grief, remained for fourteen years, until November, 1863. When it was withdrawn Neale wrote that he had 'neither withdrawn a single word nor altered a single practice'.[2]

Neale suffered persecution from his neighbours as well as from his Bishop. Malicious charges were brought against him, even including one that he had misappropriated College funds, when the truth was that he spent on the College out of his own pocket many times more than he ever received in his ludicrous salary. His opponents played on the ignorance and prejudice of the illiterate village folk. When one of the pensioners was buried with the use of a bier and a pall with a Cross on it, a mob forcibly took the coffin away from the bearers, lit fires against the building and broke windows. There were indeed several attempts to set fire to

---

[1] Letter to Bishop Gilbert, March 26, 1849. *Letters of John Mason Neale, D.D.*, p. 116. Edited by his daughter, Mary Lawson, Longmans, 1910.
[2] *Letters*, p. 328.

the College. At one time Neale had fire watchers on duty all night, and detectives on guard. The whole story, little over a century old, seems almost incredible.

Neale's humble post, when his persecutors left him alone, gave him what he most desired, time for study, research and writing. He took his share in the general Movement, attended meetings, delivered lectures, served on committees, wrote pamphlets, but he was most at home in his study among his books. He wrote voluminously: the bibliography in his *Memoir* gives the titles of 113 large and small publications issued in his life time, not counting twenty-five volumes, mostly of sermons, published in steady succession for twelve years after his death. His works included elaborate scholarly histories, books on ecclesiology and liturgiology, stories for children, and volumes of hymns. For two years he acted as leader writer for the *Morning Chronicle*. Writing to his wife in July, 1851, he exclaims, about this appointment: 'Ten guineas a week equals £546 a year, which more than doubles our income you know.' Many of his books had large sales and some brought him an income, though always a slender one. The only ecclesiastical post he was ever offered, after his resignation from Crawley, was the Provostship of the Scottish Episcopal Cathedral at Perth, which he declined on the double ground that his health was probably not good enough and that in any case he felt he ought not to leave the Church in England in the midst of the Tractarian controversy. His Doctorate, in 1860, was conferred by Hartford University in America.

In 1855 he took the momentous step of founding St Margaret's Sisterhood at East Grinstead, after characteristically thorough enquiries into the working of existing sisterhoods. The original purpose was to provide religiously trained and dedicated women with knowledge of nursing to care for the sick poor in their own homes. Sussex was then a county of isolated farms and poor cottages; poverty abounded and the most shocking sanitary conditions. Doctors and medicines were often unobtainable and the spiritual destitution matched the physical. Sussex, he said, was 'heathen to all intents and purposes'. The Sisterhood began in a small way but the numbers of these heroic and self-sacrificing women steadily grew and support for the venture increased. Neale gave himself to their spiritual care and training, conducting Bible classes and devotional services, and took a share often in their nursing work. Frequently he insisted on going off in severe wintry weather over the dreadful roads to take necessary medicines and supplies to some isolated Sister, a practice which undoubtedly shortened his life. The Sisters themselves took great risks. They often lived for long periods in the already overcrowded cottages with their patients. They saved many lives but some of them died during epidemics of diphtheria and scarlet fever. At the funeral of one Sister who had so died his persecutors struck again. Though the arrangements for the funeral at Lewes had been made by the relations, a mob assaulted Neale and some of the Sisters who had to be rescued by the police.

The impressive convent buildings at East Grinstead are a striking memorial to Neale, and the work of the Sisterhood has widened and grown in the most remarkable way. There are now several branch houses in England, Wales and Scotland and work is in progress also in Ceylon and South Africa. It takes a variety of forms, including schools and orphanages, homes for incurables, delicate children, elderly ladies, and a home for the dying.[1]

Notwithstanding his weak chest Neale was muscularly strong and just under six feet in height. He was very fond of strenuous walking, doing twenty to thirty miles a day. He had no graces as a speaker, his voice was harsh and his delivery abrupt. But he was direct and real and simple and knew how to talk to his pensioners. There is an interesting reference to him in the reminiscences of Sabine Baring Gould, the versatile, voluminous and eccentric vicar of Lew Trenchard, who counted himself in many ways as one of his disciples. 'Being shortsighted he read his sermons from a little book held close to his eyes. He preached without action and his voice had a nasal twang. He wore black whiskers and his hair rather long.' In spite of controversy and opposition, it is recorded that he was 'supremely happy' at East Grinstead, 'with his pensioners, his five children, his books, his dreams, and the great Sussex Downs'.

Neale was a great scholar, richly endowed with both linguistic and poetic gifts, sometimes approaching genius, and his life-long researches into ancient Latin and Greek hymnody made great treasures, before unknown to English readers, available to the Church. He is supreme among translators of hymns, both for the scale of his work and for the high quality of most of it. His *Collected Hymns*, published after his death, fill four hundred and

---

[1] See *The Church of England Year Book*, 1960.

sixty closely printed pages. Inevitably his muse trots at times in pedestrian fashion, but how often it takes wings! In the midst of his scholarly and propagandist labours 'he constantly went back to the translating or composition of hymns', his biographer says.[1]

Included among his publications in this field are *Hymns for Children*, 1842, which reached its tenth edition soon after his death; *Hymns for the Sick*, 1843; *Hymns for the Young*, 1844; *Mediaeval Hymns and Sequences*, 1851; *The Hymnal Noted*, 1852; *Carols for Christmas and Easter*, 1853; *The Rhythm of Bernard of Morlaix*, 1858; *Hymns of the Eastern Church*, 1862; *Hymns, chiefly Mediaeval, on the Joys and Glories of Paradise*, 1865. Though not a particularly practical book for congregational use, *The Hymnal Noted* was very influential. It was produced for the Ecclesiological Society with the Rev Thomas Helmore as musical editor, who acted in that capacity for the *Carols* also. Ninety-four of its 105 hymns were by Neale, mostly from the Sarum Office Books, with plain-song melodies. He wrote in the preface to his *Mediaeval Hymns* that 'some of the happiest and most instructive hours of my life were spent in the subcommittee' at work on the *Hymnal Noted*. From this collection come 'Now that daylight fills the sky', 'O what their joy and their glory must be', 'Before the ending of the day', 'Of the Father sole begotten', 'Light's glittering morn', and 'Come, Thou Holy Paraclete'.

Neale was a master of old Latin literature and as eager as anyone to restore the old hymns, but he was very critical of the bungling attempts of Chandler and company who had ignorantly fastened on the Paris Breviary, and wrote a 'pungent paper' about them in *The Christian Remembrancer* in 1850. His own work was to mend matters. In *Mediaeval Hymns and Sequences* he translated four hundred pages of Latin poems from a great variety of really ancient authors; among them Venantius Fortunatus, Bede, Theodulph, Peter Damian, Notker, Godescalcus, and Adam of St Victor, 'in my mind the greatest Latin poet, not only of mediaeval, but of all ages'. They come from the sixth century onwards. Here first appeared many hymns now widely used. As one turns the pages, without trying to make an exhaustive list, one notes 'The royal banners forward go', 'Sing, my tongue, the glorious battle', 'Glory, laud and honour', 'Jesus, kind above

[1] *J. M. Neale, D.D., A Memoir*, E. A. Towle, Longmans, p. 208.

all other', 'O come, O come, Emmanuel' (or, as he wrote it, 'Draw nigh, draw nigh, Emmanuel'), 'To the Name that brings salvation'.

Neale did much to introduce the Orthodox Churches to Christians in England. He was largely responsible for the foundation of the Eastern Churches Association in 1863 and worked actively to promote mutual understanding, reaching scholars through his *History of the Holy Eastern Church* and other writings, and the general public with his hymn translations. This was unexplored country and the difficulties of turning the material into English verse were much greater than with the Latin ones. He wrote in the preface to *Hymns of the Eastern Church*: 'It is a most remarkable fact and one which shows how very little interest has been hitherto felt in the Eastern Church, that these are literally, I believe, the only English versions of any part of the treasures of Oriental hymnology. . . . The eighteen quarto volumes of Greek Church poetry can only at present be known to the English reader by my little book.' He went on to explain the difficulties of translation. The Latin hymns were already in verse and one could follow the same metre, but the Greek Church has no metrical hymns: the Canons are all in prose. 'The body of the Eastern breviary is ecclesiastical poetry: poetry not strictly speaking written in verse but in measured prose.' What is the right metre to use in English? Further, the great length of the Canons makes selection inevitable. 'We have no pattern or example of any kind to direct our labour.'

In the third edition he admitted that three of the hymns contained so little from the Greek that he really ought not to have called them translations: 'Art thou weary', 'O happy band of pilgrims', and 'Safe home, safe home in port'. It seems likely that in many more instances than these Neale's mind had been set going by some scrap of Greek and he had turned out what was in effect an original hymn. That is the conclusion to be drawn from his frequent note: 'Based on . . .', and the fact that later scholars surveying the same material have often failed to discover any originals. His hymns from the Greek are inevitably more adaptations than translations, the originals providing only sparks to kindle his own poetic flame. Many now familiar hymns are to be found in these pages. In addition to the three named above there are, for example, 'Fierce was the wild billow', 'The day is past and over', 'A great and mighty wonder', from Anatolius;

'Christian, dost thou see them', from St Andrew of Crete; 'Tis the day of Resurrection', from St John Damascene, whom Neale calls the greatest of the poets of the Eastern Church; and 'Come, ye faithful, raise the strain', which Neale leaves without a name.

Some of his *Carols* have now become almost folk songs, as if they had always been ours and not really written just over a century ago. 'Good Christian men, rejoice' is based, he says, on 'a patois carol, perhaps fourteenth century.' The words of 'Good King Wenceslas' were Neale's own. He used to gather his children and the pensioners together at Christmas and Easter in the hall of Sackville College to sing both the old carols and the new ones he had written.

Children took to Neale. He had a gift for explaining things in simple words. For some twenty years he preached every Sunday evening to a little company of simple folk, old men and women and servants and children. On Sunday afternoons he spoke to the children at the orphanage. In the *Letters* (p. 297) which she edited, his daughter writes: 'I think one may safely say he never preached a dull sermon to children nor one above their heads.' He had been brought up in a strict evangelical home against whose outlook he reacted violently in later life. The very first book he wrote was *Hymns for Children*. When he was working at it in 1842 he wrote to a friend: 'Long ago I determined that if no one else did anything to free our poor children from the yoke of Watts I would try. I have been seriously at work at it the last six weeks and have accomplished a little volume of thirty-four.'[1] He intended it chiefly for use in village schools and had composed morning and evening hymns for each day in the week and some for curiously selected Christian seasons and home events. The only one in common use today is the Good Friday hymn, 'A time to watch, a time to pray'. It is not an impressive collection and Neale himself in later years criticized them as 'intolerably prosaic'. And who are we to contradict him? It may be noted here that Neale also wrote a number of stories for children which were much in demand at one time.

All later hymn books, of whatever denomination, have benefited greatly from the influence of the Oxford Movement, chiefly as mediated through Neale. *Hymns Ancient and Modern*, first published in 1861, summed up its message for hymnody. The

[1]*Letters*, p. 46.

## The Royal Banners

word 'ancient' in the title had a magical effect on its constituency and it was a tremendous success. The later *English Hymnal* went to further extremes in the invocation of the Virgin Mary and the saints. But even Free Church hymn books have gained much: many of the old hymns made available by Neale and others have been warmly welcomed and the Church's Year is more widely observed, though the Movement's sacramentarian views and the observance of saints' days have not been accepted.

Neale rejoiced in the wide use of his hymns. He thought of them always as a gift to the Church. In the preface to *Hymns on the Joys and Glories of Paradise*, published in the last year of his life, he wrote: 'Any compiler of a future hymn book is perfectly welcome to make use of anything contained in this little book. And I am glad to have the opportunity of saying how strongly I feel that a hymn, whether original or translated, ought, the moment it be published, to become the common property of Christendom, the author retaining no private right in it whatever. I suppose that no one ever sent forth a hymn without some faint hope that he might be casting his two mites into that treasury of the Church into which the "many that were rich"—Ambrose and Hildebert and Adam and Bernard of Cluny; yes, and Santeuil and Coffin—"cast in much". But having so cast it in, is not claiming a vested interest in it something like "keeping back part of the price of the land"?'

Surely in fact few in all the history of the Church have cast so much into that treasury as Neale. I find no fewer than sixty-seven of his hymns in one or more of the leading current books, fourteen of them original compositions. More than a tenth of the hymns in the *English Hymnal*, seventy-two out of 656, are his. In one edition of *Hymns Ancient and Modern* one-eighth of the contents were his work. Even the 'Protestants' he professed to scorn are gratefully in his debt. But his humility was genuine and part of the man. 'The most edifying of all his teaching to my own soul', wrote a friend, 'was when I saw him in his last illness, laying in the dust all his works and all his talents, and casting himself as a little child only on the atoning work of Jesus Christ'. He died in 1866 at the age of forty-eight. On his death bed they sang to him his own translations of the hymns of Bernard of Morlaix about that land at whose gates he was waiting, and at the funeral his own hymn, 'Safe home, safe home in port!'

# 8

# FOR ALL THE SAINTS

*William Walsham How (1823-97), the beloved bishop*

ONE of How's greatest distinctions was the number of impressive invitations that he declined. He was surprisingly offered All Saints', Margaret Street, one of the meccas of the highest Anglo-Catholics. Being himself a moderate old-fashioned High Churchman, loyal to the Prayer Book, very suspicious of any apparently Romanizing tendencies, and disliking the extravagances of the extreme ritualists, it was perhaps only an act of prudence and wisdom to decline. But he refused also the bishoprics of Natal, Cape Town, New Zealand, Montreal and Jamaica. In England he declined the livings of Brighton and Windsor, a canonry at Winchester, and the bishoprics of Manchester and Durham. Both the invitations and his refusals tell us a good deal about the man. Certainly ambition was a word with no meaning for him.

Born in 1823 in Shrewsbury, the son of a solicitor, he was educated at Wadham College, Oxford, read theology at Durham, and after a curacy at Kidderminster, became rector of Whittington, Shropshire, in 1851. In this country parish he remained for twenty-eight years. Then, rather reluctantly, he became, in 1879, Suffragan to the Bishop of London with oversight of the East End. His title, by some queer ecclesiastical necessity, was Bishop of Bedford. He often mystified his hearers, who thought he came from a rural diocese, by depicting the poverty, squalor and overcrowding of the slums where he worked!

East London was a startling contrast to his lovely country parish. He found a disheartening state of affairs. The clergy were too few and overworked, and many were discouraged. Thousands of the people, artisans, dockers, factory girls, were completely untouched by the Church and without any religion. Many were out of work and there was widespread poverty. A considerable group were professional criminals. How threw himself into his new task with vigour. Believing that the first need was to get more clergy, he started the East London Church Fund. He soon proved himself a source of spiritual inspiration to clergy and people, travelling indefatigably round the diocese by tram and bus, going everywhere, from lodginghouses to Salvation Army halls. His pastoral staff had engraved on it a motto from St Bernard which he was fond of quoting, *Pasce verbo, pasce vita,* 'Feed with the Word: feed with the Life.' He did both. In a remarkable way he won the affection of the whole community.

His love of children, who loved him heartily in return, was also a door to the affection of the parents. 'Why do you wear them things on your legs?' was a question that could not be asked of one who was at all frightening! Once he was confronted by rows of little tots, all dressed up for the bishop, and warned to be on their best behaviour for the great man, and he began by reciting Humpty Dumpty—which rapidly melted the ice. 'One of the titles I got in East London and the one I liked best was "The children's bishop" ', he said afterwards.

After six years he was offered the diocese of Manchester in 1885, a notable 'preferment', but he refused. Reluctantly in 1888 he agreed to go to Wakefield to preside over the new diocese which had just been carved out of Ripon. It was an industrial district and little improvement on East London from the point of view of amenities. He complained of 'smoke and acid fumes, raw cold, dirt'. 'There is not a garden in my diocese where I can pick a flower without blacking my fingers!' He showed here the same untiring industry and gifts of leadership, and when in 1890 he was invited to become Bishop of Durham, one of the most exalted positions in the Church of England, with an income more than double that of Wakefield, he declined. He told the Prime Minister that he could not desert his colleagues in the building up of the new diocese, and that in any case he did not possess the gifts necessary for so influential a position, or the academic distinction. So in Wakefield he stayed until his death in 1897. A contemporary describes 'the well-knit figure, crisp grey hair, the bright brown eyes, and the mouth so whimsical and sympathetic, with its trick of becoming suddenly very firm and set if he heard or saw what he did not like.'[1] His son said he lived 'a simple, joyous life', 'a song of praise to his Creator'.

He wrote many books which were famous and most useful in

---

[1] *Life of Bishop Walsham How*, F. D. How, Isbister, 1898.

their day and had a large circulation. Here we must confine attention to his contribution to hymnody which was very notable and perhaps entitles him to rank as the finest hymn writer of his century. He was joint editor with T. B. Morrell of *Psalms and Hymns*, published in 1854 with revised editions in 1864 and 1867. For long it was the most considerable rival of *Hymns Ancient and Modern*, though How was glad when the latter gained ground, as he wanted to see one book in use throughout the Church of England. He was also one of the compilers of *Church Hymns* for the SPCK with John Ellerton.[1] He wrote himself fifty-four hymns, which reach a very high level of spiritual sincerity and poetic quality. Most of them remained in wide use for many years, and ten or twelve of them are still today among our best loved and most familiar. No fewer than twenty-five are in one or more of our current books. They include hymns for most of the Christian festivals, for sacramental services, for the seasons of the year, and for children. He was in great demand as a writer of hymns for special occasions. For example, in 1897 a request came from the Prince of Wales that he would write a hymn to be sung at the sixtieth Jubilee of Queen Victoria's reign that year. The hymn he wrote was set to music by Arthur Sullivan and was immensely popular.

He kept his child-like spirit to the end, and many stories are told of his love of children's parties, his skill at writing nonsense verses, his enthusiastic support for the Waifs and Strays Society. So it is not surprising that he should have written some exceptionally good children's hymns, of which three at least are still widely used. It is interesting to find that in the latest hymn book specially prepared for children, *Sunday School Praise*, six of his hymns appear. 'It is a thing most wonderful', a quiet, thoughtful hymn for children, with I John 4.10 for text, is in seven hymnals. 'Behold a little child', concrete and full of pictures, specially meant for boys, is in four. 'Come praise your Lord and Saviour', a jubilant, vigorous song, a great favourite with children of an older generation but now a little old-fashioned in language, has survived in only one, as has 'Lord, this day Thy children meet', a simple and eminently suitable hymn which deserves better treatment. He was largely responsible for the improvements in 'Brightly gleams our banner', by E. J. Potter.

[1]See page 123.

Three of his hymns for the seasons of the year are still more or less in use: 'Summer suns are glowing' somehow itself glowing in keeping with its theme; 'Winter reigneth o'er the land'; and 'The year is swiftly waning'.

Most popular of all is his noble 'For all the saints', a triumphant, inspiring, invigorating work which is inevitably in all the hymnals. Little behind it in popularity is 'We give Thee but Thine own'. It is surely one of the best on the fundamental virtue of stewardship, stressing as it does the call to give not only money but personal service. Of similar wide use is 'To Thee our God we fly', an admirable prayer for national righteousness.

O Jesus, Thou art standing
Outside the fast-closed door.

is based on Revelation 3.20. Holman Hunt's well-known picture, more famous then than now, had its influence on the hymn, but it was first suggested by a poem by Jean Ingelow. This hymn well illustrates the ardent evangelical spirit of its author, which went most happily and naturally together with his catholicism and strong Church sense, as it often does. It is interesting that Bishop How's hymns are now more fully represented in non-Anglican hymnals than in Anglican ones.

'Soldiers of the Cross arise', found in six books, is one more evidence of How's life-long concern for those straying in sin and suffering from poverty and misery. It could have been his crusading clarion in the east London of his day, and has appealed to those in all the churches moved by a similar social concern. 'O Word of God incarnate' is one of the best hymns on the Bible, though it is chiefly used now by non-Anglicans. Less widely used are 'On wings of living light', a fine Easter hymn with true lyric qualities; 'O Jesus, strong and pure and true', written for the Jubilee of Marlborough College in 1893 and still an appealing hymn for senior boys and girls; and 'Who is this so weak and helpless', a hymn on the Incarnation, which has perhaps failed in competition with the somewhat similar 'Who is He in yonder stall' by B. R. Hanby. Several more survive now in only one or two hymnals.

It is a very deep debt that we owe to William Walsham How, who taught the way of Christ 'by word and by life'.

# 9

# THE DAY THOU GAVEST
## *John Ellerton* (1826-93), *the parish priest whose life was devoted to hymns*

A NAME to be had in high honour in hymnody is that of John Ellerton. He was a faithful and beloved parish priest, but as the great work of his life he gave himself, one might say, to the cause of hymns. He was the writer of a number of our very best; he edited and helped to edit several hymn books; he did much useful research into the history of hymns and no man has written more or better on hymnology generally. Matthew Arnold hailed him as 'the greatest of living hymnologists'.

The story of his life is soon told so far as outward events go. He was born in London on December 16, 1826, of a Yorkshire family. He was brought up in pronouncedly evangelical circles, of which he always spoke with deep respect, but when he went up to Trinity College, Cambridge, he came under the influence of F. D. Maurice. His friend, colleague and biographer, Henry Housman, says that Ellerton was never a party man. 'He always seemed to me to combine in himself the distinguishing excellency of each—the subjective piety of the Evangelical, the objective adoration of the High, the intellectual freedom of the Broad.'[1] Ill-health prevented him from taking any scholastic honours, and he just missed winning the Chancellor's Medal for an English poem.

After curacies at Easebourne in Sussex and at Brighton, he was made vicar of Crewe Green, Cheshire, on the outskirts of the railway town. He devoted himself specially to work among the men at the local railway workshops and took an active part in the management and educational programme of the Mechanics Institute, which offered what we might now call WEA classes. Here he began to write his hymns. From there he moved to the

[1] *John Ellerton*, Henry Housman, SPCK, 1896, p. 22.

## The Day Thou Gavest

little rural parish of Hinstock, Shropshire, where he gave his leisure to the study of hymnology. After five years of this seclusion he became rector of the suburban parish of Barnes, Surrey, and devoted himself with energy and enthusiasm to the varied work among the large population. This removal to the neighbourhood of London made possible an intimate share in the work of SPCK, especially in the editing of hymnals, of which more will be said. In 1884 he was obliged to resign owing to a severe attack of pleurisy which threatened his life. While recuperating he undertook light chaplaincy duties in Switzerland and Italy. Both for its own sake, and because of the light it throws on Ellerton himself, I quote the beautiful poem he wrote in those months.

> Here in this peaceful time and place of rest
>    I lift my thoughts, dear Master, unto Thee,
> Seeking in calm repose upon Thy breast
>    Some precious pledge that Thou art come with me.
>
> Thou too hast known the thronging of the crowd,
>    The 'many coming' as the hours went by,
> The weary head in deep exhaustion bowed,
>    The broken sleep, the sudden midnight cry.
>
> All these are Thine, O Bearer of our woes;
>    No rest for Thee our suffering manhood gave,
> Through Thy three years no leisure for repose,
>    Till that last Sabbath in Thy garden grave.
>
> Yet Thy compassion knows my feebler frame.
>    Mine is the rest my Master would not take;
> And if my work indeed be in Thy name,
>    These quiet hours are hallowed for Thy sake.
>
> Thou art with me; as when Thy twelve returned
>    And poured their tale of labours at Thy feet,
> Thy pitying eye their weariness discerned,
>    Thy love provided them some still retreat.
>
> With Thee they climbed the gorge whence Jordan falls,
>    Saw Hermon's snow peaks glow with dawn's red fire,
> And watched, beneath the heathen's broken walls,
>    The blue sea whitening on the shores of Tyre.
>
> Thou lovedst Thy fair land, the solitudes
>    Of her grey hills, fit home for musings high

> Spring with her glowing flowers and nestling broods,
> The moonlit garden and the sunset sky.
>
> Nor these alone; for Thou didst condescend
> The joys of human fellowship to share,
> The simple welcome of some village friend,
> Mary's deep gladness, Martha's loving care.
>
> In toil, in leisure, I may learn of Thee,
> Keep Thee beside me in my mountain walk,
> Set to Thy name the music of the sea
> And open all my heart in voiceless talk.
>
> So when Thy call shall bid me to return
> With strength renewed, to labour in my place,
> My lips shall overflow, my heart shall burn,
> With new revealings of Thy boundless grace.

In 1885 he became rector of White Roding in Essex, a post which again left him leisure for study and writing. There he wrote a book on the Holy Communion, edited one on the work of a parish priest, collected his *Hymns Original and Translated*, 1889, and worked on the editorial committee for the 1889 edition of *Hymns Ancient and Modern*. He died in June, 1893, at Torquay. He had been nominated as Canon of St Albans but ill-health prevented him from being installed. Six of his own hymns were sung at his funeral service.

It is moving to read some of the tributes paid to him by his friends. They tell of his sympathy and helpfulness as pastor, 'always making the best of and doing his best for others, never thinking of himself', writes the biographer who had been his curate through the busy years at Barnes. His impressive way of reading the Lessons is noted. He is called 'the most delightful of companions', with wide interests in archaeology, geology, butterflies, and literature. Here we are concerned to think of him as hymn-writer, hymnal editor and hymnologist.

Ninety-eight hymns and translations are listed in his biography, of which no fewer than twenty-six are in current hymnals. He always gave free permission for their use, 'regarding himself not so much as their author as the channel through which God had given them to the Church.'[1] They show a wide variety of style and theme, but are all marked by sincerity and reverence and poetic

---

[1] Housman, p. 169.

## The Day Thou Gavest 121

skill. He shrank from exaggerated sentiment. Hymns were for congregational use and must not assume too advanced a degree of spiritual experience, or indulge in subtlety of language. Hymns must never 'tempt men to come before the God of truth with superficial emotions and unreal words'.[1]

It was this that prompted his vigorous protests against the Prayer Book chopping up of the Psalms into sixty more or less equal chunks for use in public worship. 'The Book of Psalms is much more than a hymnal. It is a manual of private as well as public devotion; . . . it is an inspired record of the spiritual experiences of saints under the old covenant; it embraces compositions corresponding . . . with the historical ballads and patriotic songs of other nations. Therefore in structure it is not to be compared with any collection of hymns formed expressly for congregational use. There is absolutely no evidence whatever that the whole Psalter, as we have it, was so used by the Jewish Church. Had this been understood at the time of the Reformation, the absurdity of attempting to versify it from end to end for the congregation would have been seen.'[2] How Isaac Watts would have applauded!

'Every feeling which enters into any act of true worship may fitly find expression in a hymn. But there we must fix our limit. Hymns may express adoration, thanksgiving, commemoration of God's mercies; they may be prayers, penitential, supplicatory, intercessory; they may be devout aspirations after God; but in any case they must be forms of worship. It is not enough that they *suggest* devotion, they must be capable of *expressing* it. The observance of this rule would clear the ground at once of much irrelevant matter with which the hymn books of every church and sect are at present encumbered. The whole multitude of didactic and hortatory verses, the addresses to sinners and saints, the paraphrases of Scripture prophecies, promises and warnings, the descriptions of heaven and hell, the elaborate elucidations of the anatomy and pathology of the soul; all these, whatever be their value in the chamber, the study or the pulpit, ought utterly and for ever to be banished from the choir. Forms of common worship must express such thoughts and feelings as are, or ought to be, common to all worshippers.'[3]

As has been already noted, twenty-six of his hymns are still in

[1]Housman, p. 205.   [2]Housman, p. 226.   [3]Housman, pp. 228ff and 235.

use. We may usefully take a look at some of the best known. Three are in all eight of the current books. 'This is the day of light', an admirable hymn for public worship; 'Saviour, again to Thy dear name we raise', one of the great evening hymns; and that superb hymn of fellowship with 'the holy Church throughout all the world', 'The day Thou gavest, Lord, is ended'. Almost as widely used, in six books, is the impressive crucifixion hymn, 'Throned upon the aweful tree', which leads our thoughts beyond the physical agony of our Lord to His anguish of spirit.

Welcome because it meets a need that is not explicitly provided for elsewhere, is his hymn for a mid-day service in a city church, included in seven hymnals,

> Behold us, Lord, a little space
> From daily tasks set free.

To him we owe one of the best of the very few usable hymns for marriages, most of those on offer being spoilt by an unreal sentimentality, 'O Father, all creating'.

Ellerton has made a notable contribution in another realm also, where unreality, sentimentality and even definitely unChristian teaching are all too common, hymns on death and the future life. 'God of the living' is a splendid assertion of Christian faith, and a protest against the notion that the dead are 'wrapt in dreamless sleep profound'. This makes all the more regrettable that in another great hymn which has been used at countless funerals of the famous and the humble, he should have lapsed. 'Now the labourer's task is o'er' is a great hymn marred by the refrain

> Father, in Thy gracious keeping
> Leave we now Thy servant *sleeping*

a sentiment which is really incompatible with what the hymn itself asserts. Another hymn on the same theme, which is only in the *Church Hymnary* and the *Methodist Hymn Book,* is 'When the day of toil is done'. It was first sung at the funeral of the manager of the Crewe Railway Works, a man of promise who died at the age of thirty-five. Though it is naturally not in any hymn book today, we may recall his 'O Lord of life and death', written in 1871 in a time of pestilence, which is notable for its commonsense and courage in blaming the plague not on divine anger but on bad drainage and dirt.

A beautiful hymn of praise which seems to be coming into wider use is 'Sing hallelujah forth in duteous praise'. It is based upon the fifth-century Latin of the Mozarabic Breviary, the old

Spanish Liturgy which was supplanted by the Roman in the tenth century. A glowing and triumphant Easter hymn, worthy of wider use, is his 'Welcome, happy morning' which is not in any of the Anglican books. It is based upon a Latin poem by Venantius Fortunatus. Fortunatus was a most interesting character, a travelling troubadour who became a priest and eventually a bishop, devoting his gifts of verse writing and song to the service of the Church. He was a native of Italy, lived about 530 to 609, and was the author of another famous hymn, *Vexilla regis prodeunt*, translated by J. M. Neale as 'The royal banners forward go', and of 'Sing my tongue, the glorious battle', in Dearmer's translation.

Another of Ellerton's translations is the Christmas hymn,

> From east to west, from shore to shore,
> Let every heart awake and sing
> The holy child whom Mary bore,
> The Christ, the everlasting King.

The author of the original was Caelius Sedulius, about whom little is known. He was born in Rome, was probably converted to Christianity late in life and died about 450. His works were collected after his death and include a poem covering the whole Gospel story. The original Latin of this hymn is in many ancient breviaries.

There are many more of Ellerton's hymns which are worthy of comment and quotation, but I end with quoting a lovely brief hymn, also a translation from an unidentified source, but possibly St Ambrose. It is now only in *Hymns Ancient and Modern* and *The English Hymnal*.

> O strength and stay upholding all creation,
> Who ever dost Thyself unmoved abide,
> Yet day by day the light in due gradation
> From hour to hour through all its changes guide:
> Grant to life's day a calm unclouded ending,
> An eve untouched by shadows of decay,
> The brightness of a holy death-bed blending
> With dawning glories of the eternal day.

Ellerton was concerned in the editing of several hymnals. In 1871 he joined his friend Canon Walsham How, who was to rival his own great contributions to hymnody, in producing *Children's Hymns and School Prayers*, eight of the 153 being written by himself. In 1881 he was joint editor with Mrs Carey Brock of the more important *Children's Hymn Book*. In the preface he said that the object was 'to provide a hymnal for the young in which, whilst a high standard of excellence and a healthy religious tone are preserved, every hymn shall be, as regards the sentiments conveyed and the expressions used, within their possible experience, and as far as may be within their comprehension'. They had excluded hymns which 'however valuable and beautiful in themselves it would be impossible for children to use without a simulation of religious experience dangerous to the simplicity and truthfulness of their relations with God. . . . At the same time, they have not forgotten the necessity of making children familiar in childhood with such hymns as they can love and value all their lives'. He once wrote that it was 'simple misery' to him to hear a group of children thoughtlessly singing 'Abide with me'.

He had a very large share in the production of *Church Hymns* for the SPCK, being joint editor with Walsham How and Berdmore Compton. In a long letter written when it was being planned it is most impressive to note his ideas as to the range of choice open to them. He pled for the inclusion of ancient Latin, Greek and mediaeval hymns and equally for hymns by living authors. He urged investigation of the possibilities of German, Danish and French Protestant hymns, while Watts and Doddridge must not be forgotten. He contributed eleven originals and nine translations of his own to the volume, which was published in 1871. From the outset he had asked for a companion to be produced with notes on the hymns and their authors and was encouraged to go ahead. The work of preparing such notes on each of the six hundred hymns 'occupied very pleasantly', he said, 'such leisure time as could be given to it during nine years of a busy life'. His successors in the same field have profited by his researches.

The compilers of *Hymns Ancient and Modern* had frequently consulted him, but he had not liked their first edition in 1861 and had agreed to join in the production of *Church Hymns*. But in 1885 he was drawn into the inner circle and became one of the committee that prepared the 1889 edition. Yet he must have been sympathetic from the start with at least one of their aims, a reduction in the number of competing books. In an article written by Ellerton in 1864 he described the state of Anglican hymnody as 'chaotic'. 'None has authorized the use of any hymn book whatever, though most of our bishops have now recommended, or at least approved, some one or more; the field is open to unrestricted competition. . . . Each clergyman may compile a fresh hymn book for his own congregation if he have time, money and patience. The five or six best known selections . . . have each its following of enthusiastic supporters.'[1]

The promoters of *Hymns Ancient and Modern*, notably Sir H. W. Baker, had gathered together some twenty people, including the editors of several existing hymn books, who agreed to give up their own in favour of a joint volume. The first edition in 1861 contained only 273 hymns, but several supplements and revised editions appeared from time to time. The revision of 1875 with 473 hymns contained thirteen by Ellerton and, as we have said, he was drawn into the preparation of the 1889 edition, which included twenty-six of his. The chairman of the committee wrote that 'it would be scarcely possible to exaggerate the value of the assistance which was rendered by Mr Ellerton in the production of the complete edition'.

Ellerton was one of the editors of the *London Mission Hymn Book*, for use in a General London Mission in 1884, and of the *Temperance Hymn Book*. He helped with the *Hymnal Companion to the Book of Common Prayer*. 'In fact,' writes his biographer, 'it is no exaggeration to say that his hand may be traced and his voice heard in every hymn book and important publication during the last thirty years,' that is, before 1896 and in the Church of England, 'while no less than eighty-six hymns, original and translated, proceeded from his pen'.[2]

Ellerton was devoted to hymns from his first curacy to his death bed. In 1879 he spoke of 'more than twenty years devoted to hymnology'. In his last days as an invalid at Torquay he was greatly interested in Julian's massive *Dictionary of Hymnology* which had just been published. 'When lying half-conscious on his death bed, hymn after hymn flowed from his lips in a never-ending stream.'

---

[1] Housman, p. 192. Julian lists seventy-eight Anglican hymn books produced between 1820 and 1850.
[2] Housman, p. 178.

# 10

## THE CONTRIBUTION OF WOMEN

THE churches have been very slow to accord to women that opportunity for equal ministry which should be theirs both on the ground of ability and of the fundamental Christian truth as to their equal standing in the sight of God. Some Churches behave rather better than others, and at least do not seek to defend their practice by spurious theological arguments, but nearly all still lag sadly behind commerce and the professions in the opportunities they offer. Women have still to struggle against irrational regulations and prejudices, not least on the part of women themselves. This is, of course, no question of 'women's rights', which is quite the wrong line of thought, but of recognition of God-given endowments and of according to them equal opportunity to serve God in His Church.

One of the many realms in which women have demonstrated their spiritual insight and ability to serve is hymnody. If the contributions of women were removed from our hymn books they would be very seriously depleted. I have examined from this point of view the eight current books constantly in mind in these pages, and find that, while they vary somewhat among themselves, on the average one in ten to one in eight of their authors are women. In these books no fewer than 149 women writers are represented: a much larger proportion than is generally realized. Some of our most familiar and best loved hymns are by women: to give only a few examples, 'At the name of Jesus', 'Just as I am', 'Our blest Redeemer', 'All things bright and beautiful', 'Take my life', 'Once in royal David's city'. Women have been prominent in three respects in English hymnody: they were among the pioneers; they have made a special contribution to children's hymns, as is natural; and they are among the greatest of hymn translators.

Many of our women writers were invalids, partly because of the unnatural and unhealthy lives of idleness and seclusion led by too many women in well-to-do homes in the eighteenth and nineteenth centuries. Their hymns are apt to have a sad and sombre note, to indulge too much in introspection, and to find the heart of religion in resignation and submission. To this generalization there are, as we shall see, some notable exceptions, such as Caroline Noel and Cecil Frances Alexander. Many are known today through only one hymn, as indeed are many men.

One of the first women to write and publish hymns, and the first to make a contribution of any note, was Anne Steele, 1716-1778, who is still represented in the modern books, especially by her hymn on the Bible, 'Father of mercies, in Thy Word'.[1] She was a Baptist and belonged to the Baptist Church at Broughton in Hampshire, which had a history going back to Commonwealth days, in which her family had had a great part. Her great uncle had been its lay pastor for forty years, and was succeeded by her father who held the office for some sixty years. He also was a layman, the family owning a prosperous timber business. The death of her fiancé by drowning only a few hours before the time for their wedding gave her a shock from which she never fully recovered. In 1760 she published two volumes of *Poems on Subjects chiefly Devotional* under the name of 'Theodosia'. These were mostly hymns and won quick and wide acceptance. They were extensively used in nonconformist books in Britain and America and several were included in Anglican collections. In a collected edition published in 1863, there are 144 hymns, numerous versions of psalms, and some poems with a Memoir. Her work inspired the production in 1769 of one of the earliest English hymn books, edited by two Baptist ministers, John Ash of Pershore, and Caleb Evans of Bristol. It contained sixty-two of her hymns with many by Watts and others, and had a large circulation, reaching its tenth edition by 1827.

Anne Steele's hymns reach a high general level. They are of the same type as those of Watts and Doddridge, and bear comparison well, though few are to be compared with their best. Lord Selborne justly described her as, after Doddridge, 'the most popular and perhaps the best of the followers of Watts'. Some indeed read like expressions of the conventional piety of the age, forsaking this 'vain world' and 'dark abode of clay', and longing for a better

---

[1] Two earlier women hymn writers were Anna Trapnell, a Fifth Monarchist, who published in 1654 *The Cry of a Stone: prayers and spiritual songs*, and the eccentric Anne Dutton, wife of a Baptist minister, who published hymns in 1734. Some account of her is given in *The Life and Faith of the Baptists*, by H. Wheeler Robinson, Methuen, pp. 52-60.

world on high. This morbid dissatisfaction with life no doubt in part reflects the state of her health, but one cannot help wondering if much of it is honestly felt. It must not be forgotten before passing judgment that death was a much closer reality and the expectation of life much less in her generation than today, when our religion by reaction tends to be too 'this-worldly'. Happily she has others of a very different quality, such as 'Father of mercies', mentioned above, and 'Father, whate'er of earthly bliss', which is in *Hymns Ancient and Modern*. It is not generally familiar and deserves quotation as illustrating her best work.

> Father, whate'er of earthly bliss
>   Thy sovereign will denies,
> Accepted at Thy throne of grace
>   Let this petition rise.
>
> Give me a calm and patient heart,
>   From every murmur free;
> The blessings of Thy grace impart,
>   And let me live to Thee.
>
> Let the sweet hope that Thou art mine,
>   My path of life attend;
> Thy presence through my journey shine
>   And crown my journey's end.

Anne Steele was followed by a host of women hymn-writers, so many indeed that attention in this chapter must be confined mainly to the eight who are represented in all eight of the modern books. These eight are Sarah Adams, Cecil Frances Alexander, Henriette Auber, Charlotte Elliott, Frances Ridley Havergal, Caroline Noel, Christina Rossetti, and Catherine Winkworth. But some who fall just short of that distinction should be at least mentioned for the sake of honour and that we may realize what we owe. We do well to remember Jane Borthwick and F. E. Cox, translators; Mary Maude of 'Thine for ever, God of love'; Dorothy Gurney of 'O perfect love'; Annie Hawks of 'I need Thee every hour'; Dora Greenwell of 'I am not skilled to understand'; Adelaide Procter of 'My God, I thank Thee who hast made'; Fanny Crosby or van Alstyne, the blind writer of many 'Gospel hymns'; Mary Byrne and Eleanor Hull, joint authors of 'Be Thou my vision'; Isabel Stevenson of 'Holy Father in Thy mercy'; and Mary Duncan of 'Jesus, tender Shepherd'. The list could be greatly

## The Contribution of Women

extended, but we must pass on to the illustrious eight.[1]

After Anne Steele were two other pioneers born in the eighteenth century, Henriette Auber, 1773-1862,[2] and Charlotte Elliott, 1789-1871. Henriette Auber was descended from Pierre Aubert, a refugee from the revocation of the Treaty of Nantes in 1685. She was the daughter of the rector of Tring, Herts., and spent her life in the village of Hoddesdon, close to where the well-known conference estate of High Leigh now is. Her memory was cherished in the neighbourhood for many years. She edited *The Spirit of the Psalms,* 1829, a collection of hymns on the Psalms, including a number of her own. Among them was 'Our blest Redeemer', the only one of hers that has survived in common use. By general consent it is one of the greatest of Whitsuntide hymns and has been translated into many languages. C. H. Spurgeon used some of her versions of the Psalms in *Our Own Hymn Book,* used in the Metropolitan Tabernacle and in churches ministered to by his students.

Charlotte Elliott came of a noted Evangelical family and was a grand-daughter of the famous Henry Venn. She was a well educated and cultured woman with wide interests in art and music. A severe illness in 1821 turned her into a confirmed invalid, but though she endured much suffering she lived to the age of eighty-two. In spite of her upbringing her religion had not meant much until in 1822 a visitor to her home in Clapham asked her if she was a Christian. At first she resented the question but it was the occasion of a complete change in her outlook. The visitor was Cesar Malan, one of the leaders of the evangelical movement in the Swiss Reformed Church, and a prolific writer of French hymns.

In 1834 she undertook the production of an annual, *The Christian Remembrancer Pocket Book,* and she also edited *The Invalid's Hymn Book,* 1834-41, to which she contributed over 100 hymns. Like most of her books it was issued anonymously. She also contributed to *Psalms and Hymns,* 1836, edited by her

---

[1]Reference may be made to an interesting chapter on 'Women Hymn Writers' in *Hymns and Human Life* by Dr Erik Routley, John Murray, 1952.

[2]The name is usually given as Harriet but the records at Somerset House reveal that she was christened Henriette, for which the French background of the family is no doubt responsible.

brother, Henry Venn Elliott. Other books were *Hours of Sorrow Cheered and Comforted*, 1837, *Hymns for a Week*, 1842, and *Thoughts in Verse*, 1869. When her home was broken up by death she moved to Torquay with her surviving sister for fourteen years and then to Brighton. Her best known hymn, 'Just as I am', was written when she was distressed at her inability to engage in active Christian service. She headed it 'John 6.37'. It is a very fine statement of evangelical faith. After the death of the poet Wordsworth's daughter, Dora, her husband wrote to Miss Elliott to say how greatly the hymn had helped her in her last illness. 'I do not think,' he wrote, 'Mr Wordsworth could bear to have it repeated in his presence but he is not the less sensible of the solace it gave to his one and matchless daughter.' Her grave in Grasmere has a lamb carved on the stone and the words 'O Lamb of God, I come'. More than a thousand letters thanking her for the hymn were found among Charlotte Elliott's papers after her death.

Almost as well known is 'Christian, seek not yet repose'. Surprise has been expressed at the introduction of the guardian angel in this hymn in view of its writer's evangelical outlook, and in several books the line has been altered to read, 'Cast thy dreams of ease away'. 'My God and Father, while I stray' is another that has achieved wide use in spite of its gloomy outlook. She wrote: 'Our heavenly Father knows, He and He alone, what it is day after day, and hour after hour, to fight against bodily feelings of almost overpowering weakness and languor and exhaustion, to resolve as He enables me to do, not to yield to the slothfulness, the depression, the instability, such a body causes me to long to indulge, but to rise every morning determined on taking this for my motto, "If any man will come after me, let him deny himself and take up the Cross daily and follow Me".' We may sympathize deeply with her experience, but that does not justify the use in public worship of a hymn which identifies the misfortunes and sufferings of life and none of its joys with the will of God, and interprets the phrase in the Lord's Prayer as a sigh of resignation, instead of as a prayer for the coming of God's Kingdom of love and joy and peace. Most of her hymns are indeed more suitable for private devotion than for public worship. Others in use today are 'My God, is any hour so sweet' and 'There is a holy sacrifice'.

'Nearer my God to Thee', the famous hymn based on Jacob's dream at Bethel (Gen. 28.10-22) was written by Sarah Fuller Adams, 1805-48. She was the daughter of Benjamin Flower, a radical journalist, editor of the weekly *Cambridge Intelligencer* and the monthly *Political Review*. The family was Baptist. There were two daughters, Eliza, a gifted musician, and Sarah. Sarah became a member of the Unitarian Church at South Place, Finsbury, and when her minister, the Rev W. J. Fox, edited a volume of *Hymns and Anthems*, 1841, she contributed thirteen hymns and her sister sixty-three tunes. Sarah married William Bridges Adams, a successful civil engineer and the author of several professional volumes. Robert Browning was one of their friends and he declared that Sarah was 'a very remarkable person'. Eliza died of consumption in 1846, and Sarah, who had nursed her, two years later. They are buried in the Baptist churchyard in Harlow, Essex. Another of her hymns, 'He sendeth suns, He sendeth showers', which was sung at her funeral, was in use until recently, and another, 'Part in peace', is in the Presbyterian *Church Hymnary*.

Caroline Maria Noel, 1817-77, is another writer who is remembered by one hymn only, but that one is known and valued by all the Churches, 'At the name of Jesus', based on Philippians 2.5-11. She reluctantly changed the first line to 'In the name of Jesus' to avoid the implication that she merely meant genuflection at the word. She meant adoration at contemplation of the person of Jesus as the manifestation of the Divine nature and glory. Caroline Noel was the daughter of Canon G. T. Noel and the niece of the Rev Baptist Noel, who left the Church of England to become a Baptist minister, and a very prominent one. In contrast to many introspective hymns by women this is strong, outward looking, and theologically didactic, though the full title of the book from which it comes is *The Name of Jesus and other verses for the Sick and Lonely*.

According to the *Encyclopedia of Religion and Ethics* the first man to publish a collection of English hymns for children was a certain Abraham Cheare, a Baptist minister of Plymouth, who died in prison in 1668. His verses are dismissed as 'unmitigated doggerel' though he did 'excellent work' as a pioneer.[1] In an earlier chapter we discussed Isaac Watts' work in this field, by no means without merit but still cautiously feeling his way, as he himself said. Charles Wesley was less successful in understanding

---

[1] Article on Hymns in Vol. VII by T. G. Crippen. See also article 'Children's Hymns' in Julian's *Dictionary*.

the child mind, and Neale did not shine here with his accustomed brilliance. It was not until women entered the field that real progress began to be made. The advent of two sisters, Jane and Ann Taylor, provided verses and hymns which seem almost for the first time to look at life from the child's point of view. Jane was twenty and Ann was twenty-two. Their success lies in their very simplicity and artlessness.

> Thank you, pretty cow, that made
> Pleasant milk to soak my bread,
> Every day and every night,
> Warm and fresh and sweet and white.

Here is a charming hymn, still happily to be found in some books:

> Lord, I would own Thy tender care
>     And all Thy love to me;
> The food I eat, the clothes I wear,
>     Are all bestowed by Thee.
>
> 'Tis Thou preservest me from death
>     And dangers every hour.
> I cannot draw another breath
>     Unless Thou give me power.
>
> Kind angels guard me every night,
>     As round my bed they stay:
> Nor am I absent from Thy sight
>     In darkness or by day.
>
> My health and friends and parents dear
>     To me by God are given.
> I have not any blessing here
>     But what is sent from heaven.
>
> Such goodness, Lord, and constant care
>     A child can ne'er repay;
> But may it be my daily prayer
>     To love Thee and obey.

And most of us are familiar with 'Great God and wilt Thou condescend', another beautifully simple and direct hymn.

Ann, 1782-1866, and Jane, 1783-1824, were daughters of Isaac Taylor, an artist, who trained them to do engraving. He was later ordained and became minister of Congregational churches at Colchester and Ongar successively. In 1805 the sisters jointly published *Original Poems for Infant Minds by several Young Persons,* containing mostly their own work. It was a great success, was published also in America and translated into German and Dutch. At least fifty editions appeared in this country. Two similar volumes, *Rhymes for the Nursery,* and *Original Hymns for the Use of Children,* came later. Many of their rhymes were familiar in nurseries for generations and their work started a new era in children's books.

Ann married the Rev Joseph Gilbert, a Congregational minister, in 1813, and the bringing up of a family prevented her from doing much more writing. Jane went with her invalid brother Isaac to Ilfracombe and later to Marazion in Cornwall to take care of him. She produced rather more ambitious and 'grown-up' stories, essays and poems. Her collected letters reveal an attractive, rather over-solemn, person, who yet had 'a taste for drollery', as she expressed it, which puts in its appearance at intervals. Altogether she strikes one as a lively, intelligent and happy young woman. Her preoccupation with death and the next world, which she shared with so many in her generation, is not surprising when her own letters make clear the scourge of consumption and the shockingly large number of young deaths among her close friends. The Taylors were a devoted, highly talented and affectionate family, who should be remembered with gratitude.

But supreme among hymn-writers for children, and very high on the roll of hymn-writers in general, is Cecil Frances Alexander, 1818-95. Even those of her hymns that are now dated and obsolete helped to pave the way to better things. Born in Wicklow, the daughter of Major John Humphreys, a well-to-do land owner, in 1850 she married the Rev William Alexander, then in charge of a remote parish among the bogs and hills of County Tyrone. In 1867 he became Bishop of Derry and Raphoe and after her death, Archbishop of Armagh and Primate of Ireland. She is said to have been 'an ideal clergyman's wife' in her intense interest in the services of the Church and all the life of the parish, and her devoted care of any in need.

Altogether she wrote about two hundred hymns and two hundred poems. In 1848, before her marriage, she published *Hymns for Little Children,* with a preface by John Keble, who praised their 'true poetry'. A small book of some thirty pages it had a remarkable sale and went into a hundred editions. She set herself to explain to children the articles of the Apostles' Creed, and part of her success is her ability to understand the questions children ask. 'Where was Jesus born?' 'Once in royal David's city' is the answer. 'Why did He have to die?' She replies in 'There is a green hill far away'. 'Who made the world?' 'All things bright and beautiful' is her response. She uses simple picture language, with concrete imagery and not abstract ideas. There is no morbidity or introspection. 'A namby-pamby style is most unpleasing to children, especially to boys; it is surprising how soon they can understand and follow a high order of poetry (always supposing it is not subtle or metaphysical) especially when it assumes a narrative form and has the aid of rhyme.' These are her own wise words in the preface to the *Sunday Book of Poetry* which she edited.

'All things bright and beautiful' is an admirably simple and objective hymn. It also illustrates in its original form one of the ways in which Mrs Alexander's hymns tend to become dated. The setting of her life and the times in which she lived made it natural for her to think in terms of the rich helping the poor and of a graded social order. Few now would write:

>The rich man in his castle,
>The poor man at his gate,
>God made them, high or lowly,
>And ordered their estate.

But why did she ever write that dreadful hymn, 'Within the churchyard side by side'? She has herself supplied a much better approach for children to the question of the future life in 'Every morning the red sun'.

We must not forget that Mrs Alexander was not only a writer for children. 'Jesus calls us' is a treasure for all the Churches, and growing in popularity with us all is that great and stirring hymn, 'I bind unto myself today,' where she put into verse a prose translation of an ancient Irish rhyme. It is doubtful if St Patrick had anything to do with the original, which scholars assign to the eighth century, whereas the probable dates for Patrick are 385-461.[1] The story is that Patrick sang this at Tara where he was celebrating with his little company his first Easter in Ireland and was threatened by the High King and his Druids. When he saw the soldiers and chariots he sang the Twentieth Psalm, 'Some trust in chariots and some in horses, but we will remember the name of the Lord our God'. Then, says the story, he sang this 'Lorica' or breast plate, 'at once an incantation, a war song, and a prayer'.

[1] See *Ancient Irish Poetry*, K. Meyer, Constable, p. 112.

Also widely used is her Ascension hymn, 'The golden gates are lifted up', and some half-dozen others are in use, mainly in Anglican books. Mrs Alexander's friends included Matthew Arnold and Tennyson, who thought her poem, 'The Burial of Moses', one of the best in the language and wished he had written it himself.

Christina Georgina Rossetti, 1830-94, was not by intention a hymn-writer at all, but four of her exquisite lyrics are in several books while *Songs of Praise,* in which Dearmer often allowed his love of poetry to include verses not really suitable for public worship, has seven. Altogether twelve of her poems are in one or other of our current hymn books. She is the greatest of our women poets, with the possible exception of Mrs Browning, with whom in mind and manner she is in striking contrast. Both of them wrote too much, as nearly all poets do, or allowed too much to survive. In her collected poems, edited by her brother, William Michael Rossetti, 172 pages are occupied by devotional poems, many of which had been better left unresurrected. Her two best known volumes of poetry are *Goblin Market,* 1862, and *The Prince's Progress,* 1866. Her poems are mostly personal and introspective, graceful and with deep feeling. As Walter de la Mare says, 'She asks, Am I saved? rather than, Are you?' She has a happy gift of phrase and there is a kind of magic in her best writing, a touch of what it was once the fashion to call the 'numinous'.

Those most widely used as hymns are 'In the bleak midwinter', 'Love came down at Christmas', 'The shepherds had an angel', and 'None other Lamb'. Others that appear in one or more books are 'O Christ, my God, who seest the unseen', 'O ye who taste that love is sweet', 'Sooner or later: yet at last', 'Love is the key of life and death', 'Spring bursts today', 'What are these that glow from afar?' 'Service and strength', 'Who has seen the wind'. One may be quoted in part to illustrate the quality and feel of her work for those to whom it is not familiar:

> Sooner or later: yet at last
> The Jordan must be past.
>
> Sooner or later: yet one day
> We all must pass that way,
>
> Each man, each woman, humbled, pale,
> Pass veiled within the veil.

> I rated to the full amount,
> Must render mine account
>
> When mysteries shall be revealed,
> All secrets be unsealed;
>
> I plead Thyself with Thee, I plead
> Thee in our utter need;
>
> Jesus, most merciful of men,
> Show mercy on us then;
>
> Lord God of mercy and of men,
> Show mercy on us then.

Her whole life was coloured by her profound evangelical faith. She broke off her engagement because her fiancé became a Roman Catholic, and years later she refused to become engaged to another man whom she deeply loved and continued to love all her life, because he was an agnostic. She was the daughter of two Italian refugees and her father earned a poor living as a language teacher. One of her brothers was Dante Gabriel Rossetti and she sat as model on several occasions to him and his fellow pre-Raphaelites. For a short time she taught, partly in schools conducted by her mother. Her health was always precarious. She was seriously ill with thyroid gland trouble for two years and never fully recovered from its effects. In 1892 she had an operation for cancer, of which she died two years later. Most of her life she was financially dependent on her brother William Michael, though legacies and literary earnings made her modestly comfortable in her later years.

Another woman who is among our greatest hymn-writers is Frances Ridley Havergal, 1836-79. She was the youngest child of the Rev William Henry Havergal, vicar of St Nicholas, Worcester, who did much to improve the quality of church music and himself wrote a hundred hymns and forty tunes, some of which are still in use. She lost her mother when she was eleven. A lively, attractive and precocious child, she had great gifts as player and singer. She spent a year studying in Germany and became proficient in several modern languages as well as being a student of Greek and Hebrew. She published several volumes of verse, including many hymns. When people spoke of her cleverness and 'her gifted pen' she used to say that all she did was to put down lines as God gave them to her and that she could never sit down on purpose to compose verses.

## The Contribution of Women

She had a wide circle of friends and must have been a wonderful person. There was a child-like simplicity and sincerity about her, as there is in her hymns. She was an un-selfconscious personal evangelist, and active in many forms of Christian work. This is well illustrated by her own account of the writing of 'Take my life', one of her most widely used hymns. She had been successful in leading to decision for Christ several members of the household in which she was staying. 'I was too happy to sleep and passed most of the night in praise and renewal of my own consecration. These little couplets formed themselves and chimed in my heart one after another, till they finished with "Ever, only, all for Thee" '.[1]

Sixteen of her hymns are in one or other of the current denominational hymn books. If the undenominational evangelistic collections were taken into account the number would be much larger. Her first hymn, 'Thy life was given for me' was written at Düsseldorf at the age of twenty-one. The most widely used, next to 'Take my life', is 'Lord, speak to me that I may speak'. Others included are: 'In full and glad surrender', 'Master, speak', 'Jesus, Master, whose I am', 'Who is on the Lord's side?', 'True hearted, whole hearted', 'Golden harps are sounding', and 'I could not do without Thee'.

Four women are prominent among the translators who have done so much to enrich our hymnody. Frances Elizabeth Cox, 1812-97, played a considerable part in introducing German hymns to British churches through her *Sacred Hymns from the German*, 1841, and *Hymns from the German*, 1864. Four of her translations are widely used: 'Sing praise to God', from J. J. Schutz; 'Jesus lives', from C. F. Gellert; 'O let him whose sorrow', from Heinrich Oswald; and 'Who are those like stars appearing?' from H. T. Schenk.

Jane (1813-97) and Sarah (1823-1907) Borthwick (later Mrs Findlater) not only wrote original hymns which are still in use, but jointly published four volumes of *Hymns from the Land of Luther*, 1854-62. The title furnished the initials by which they signed their writings—H. L. L. They were members of the Free Church of Scotland and widely loved and honoured. Jane is best known today by 'Jesus still lead on', from Count Zinzendorf, and 'The day departs', from Freylinghausen. Her original hymn,

---

[1] *Memorials*, p. 133.

'Come, labour on', is in several books. Sarah is remembered by her rendering of Spitta's 'O happy home'.

But the queen of hymn translators is Catherine Winkworth, 1827-78. Her only possible rival in translations from the German is John Wesley and she far surpassed him in quantity. With Frances Cox and the Borthwick sisters she introduced to English readers the treasures of German hymnody, largely inaccessible before their work. The memorial to her in Bristol Cathedral says she thus 'opened a new source of light, consolation and strength in many thousand homes'. Her *Lyra Germanica* 1855 and 1858, is of outstanding value. In the preface to the first volume she expressed 'the hope that these utterances of Christian piety which have comforted and strengthened the hearts of many true Christians in their native country may speak to the hearts of some among us, to help and cheer those who must strive and suffer, and to make us feel what a deep and true Communion of Saints exists among all the children of God in different churches and lands'. She published also *The Chorale Book for England*, 1863, and *Christian Singers of Germany*, 1869.

Most of her life was spent in the neighbourhood of Alderley Edge, Manchester, but in her later years she lived in Bristol. She was a pioneer in the higher education of women and helped in the creation of Bristol University College. A greatly gifted woman, she was a close friend of Mazzini, F. D. Maurice, Charles Kingsley, Mrs. Gaskell, Charlotte Bronte, and other distinguished figures of her day. Bishop Percival of Hereford, who was headmaster of Clifton College when she lived in Bristol, wrote: 'She was a person of remarkable intelligence and social gifts and very unusual attainments; but what specially distinguished her was her combination of rare ability and great knowledge with a certain tender and sympathetic refinement.'

Among her translations are some of our most treasured hymns. No fewer than thirty-three are to be found in our current books. 'Now thank we all our God' is in them all, a great hymn of thanksgiving which is widely used in many lands beyond that of its origin. Martin Rinckart, 1586-1649, was poet, dramatist and musician. In 1617 he became minister in his native town of Eilenburg in Germany where he remained during the grim times of the Thirty Years' War. The town became a refugee centre and endured famine and pestilence. Rinckart was its only minister of religion and spent himself and his possessions in the service of others. Many stories were told of his courageous dealings with the occupying troops. It is against that dark background that the hymn must be read. S. H. Moore has finely written: 'When hope was dead, civic security annihilated, personal ambition crushed out of existence, and when violence, famine and plague knocked at the door . . . one source alone remained whence strength could be drawn to face such dire calamity. . . . It was to that source of strength eternal that Heermann and Gerhardt and Rinckart, Flemming and Rist, Stegmann and Löwenstern, now turned.'[1] The legend that his hymn was written to celebrate the Peace of Westphalia is unfounded. It was actually printed in 1636, twelve years earlier, and Rinckart said he wrote it seven years before that.

Equally well known is 'Praise to the Lord, the almighty', which Catherine Winkworth translated from the original of Joachim Neander, 1650-80. After a wild student life, Neander was converted by the minister of St Martin's Church, Bremen, to whom he later became colleague. He was then appointed headmaster of a school in Düsseldorf where his zealous evangelism provoked such opposition that he had to leave. He returned to his old post in Bremen but met with resentment there too. He died a year later, aged thirty. He had great gifts as poet and musician and wrote some sixty hymns with tunes.

'Deck thyself, my soul, with gladness' is taken from the writing of Johann Franck, 1618-77, who had a great reputation as a poet. He was a lawyer in his native town of Guben in Brandenburg, of which he became burgomaster. The original hymn is said to be still widely used in Germany, especially at Communion services.

'Jesus, priceless treasure' is a translation of another of Franck's hymns, too intense and intimate for use in congregational worship, but nevertheless to be found in many books.

Paul Gerhardt, 1607-76, was the author of the original of the fine Christmas hymn, 'All my heart this night rejoices'. Eighty-four of his hymns have one or more English versions, including twenty by Catherine Winkworth. He is said to rank next to Luther among Lutheran hymn-writers. Dr Schweitzer in his book

---

[1] *Sursum Corda*, p. 22, an admirable series of studies of German hymn writers.

*J. S. Bach*[1] calls him 'The king of hymn-writers'. He too lived through the Thirty Years War. The cheerful, personal faith of his hymn is characteristic of his message.

The original of 'Christ the Lord is risen again' is in a hymn book of the Bohemian Brethren of 1531, but this in its turn is based upon a much older German hymn found as early as the twelfth century. Also very widely used in this country is 'O Love who formedst me to wear' from the original of J. Scheffler, 1624-77. Scheffler was a physician of eminence and a mystic. Originally a Lutheran he became a Roman Catholic priest, adopting the name of Angelus, after a Spanish mystic, and was known as Angelus Silesius, from his native country.

Such a survey of only a few of the best known of Catherine Winkworth's translations is sufficient to remind us of the immense debt all the Churches owe to her inspired work. And this whole chapter has only touched upon some of the outstanding examples of the contribution which women have made to our English hymnody.

---

[1] English edition, p. 12.

# INDEX

Academies, Dissenting, 11, 27, 29
Adams, Sarah, 130f
Addison, 93
Alexander, Cecil, 133ff
Auber, Henriette, 129
Austin, John, 18

Baptists, hymns among, 14, 18, 93, 127, 131
Barton, W., 13f
Baxter, Richard, 18, 31
Beddome, Benjamin, 93
Benson, L. F., 18, 21, 43, 50, 103
Bett, Henry, 44, 51, 55
Bonar, Horatius, 95ff
Borthwick, Jane and Sarah, 137f

Calvinism, 23, 52f, 73ff
Carols, 112
Caswall, E., 105
Chandler, J., 103, 110
Cheare, Abraham, 131
Children's hymns, 20f, 112, 116, 123f, 131ff
Church of England, hymns in, 15, 36f, 63, 90f, 102f, 124f
Communion hymns, 26, 88, 97
Conder, Josiah, 14
Congregationalists, Hymns among, 13ff
Cotterill, Thomas, 90f
Coverdale, 17
Cowper, W., 19, 57ff, 94
Cox, Frances, 137

Crashaw, 17
Crossman, 17f

Dissenting Deputies, 29f
Doddridge, Philip, 22, 27ff, 59, 62, 93

Ellerton, John, 19, 50, 66, 90, 118ff
Elliott, Charlotte, 129f

Faber, F. W., 102, 104
Faussett, Hugh, 60, 64, 73, 75
Fortunatus, 123
Franck, Johann, 139
Future Life, Hymns on, 25f, 38ff, 122, 134

Gerhardt, Paul, 45, 139
German hymns, 43ff, 137ff
Greek hymns, 111f

Harcourt, Archbishop, 91
Havergal, Frances, 136f
Herbert, George, 17
Housman, A. E., 20
How, W. W., 114ff

Johnson, Samuel, 13, 19, 21, 56, 92
Julian's *Dictionary*, 15, 23, 34, 47, 77, 85f, 131

Keach, Benjamin, 18
Keble, 100ff
Ken, 18, 92

Latin hymns, 103, 105, 110ff, 122f

# Index

Lay hymn writers, 86

Manning, Bernard, 9, 24, 45, 48
Mant, Richard, 103, 105
Mason, John, 18
Methodism, hymns in, 41ff
Missionary hymns, 25, 31, 36, 86f
Montgomery, James, 81ff
Moore, Sydney, 44f, 139
Moravians, 31, 43f, 81ff

Neale, J. M., 47, 105ff
Neander, Joachim, 139
Newman, J. H., 102ff
Newton, John, 61ff
Nicholson, Norman, 67f
Noel, Caroline, 131
Nuttall, G., 33

Oakeley, F., 104
*Olney Hymns,* 63ff, 94, 104
Orton, Job, 30, 33f
Oxford Movement, 100ff

Palgrave, F. T., 19, 65
Paraphrases, Scottish, 34, 38f
Patrick, John, 15
Payne, E. A., 31
Psalms, metrical, 13, 15ff, 121

Rinckart, Martin, 138f
Rippon, J., 14
Rossetti, Christina, 135f
Routley, E. K., 37, 65, 86, 129

Saintsbury, G., 20, 67
Sampson, G., 20, 22, 56
Scheffler, J., 140
Sedulius, 123
Selborne, Lord, 26, 65, 127
Steele, Anne, 127f
Sternhold and Hopkins, 13, 17

Tate and Brady, 13, 17, 37
Taylor, Ann and Jane, 132f
Thomas, Gilbert, 68, 77

Watts, Isaac, 9ff, 27, 46f, 48, 50, 52, 55, 92f, 112
Wesley, Charles, 9, 24, 41ff, 93, 131
Wesley, John, 9, 15, 32, 41ff
Williams, Isaac, 102, 105
Winkworth, Catherine, 138f
Wiseman, Luke, 50, 56
Wither, George, 17
Women hymn writers, 126ff
Wordsworth, 64, 71, 130

Zinzendorf, 43f

www.ingramcontent.com/pod-product-compliance
Lightning Source LLC
Chambersburg PA
CBHW051403290426
44108CB00015B/2140